ZONDERVAN'S
GREAT BIBLE TRIVIA
WORKOUT

ZONDERVAN'S
GREAT
BIBLE TRIVIA
WORKOUT

brad densmore
Illustrations by Ron Miller

GRAND RAPIDS, MICHIGAN 49530 USA

Zondervan's Great Bible Trivia Workout
Copyright © 2003 by Brad Densmore

Requests for information should be addressed to:
Zondervan, *Grand Rapids, Michigan 49530*

ISBN: 0-310-25195-8

This edition printed on acid-free paper.

Illustrations by Ron Wheeler
Interior Design by Susan Ambs

Printed in the United States of America

03 04 05 06 07 08 09 /❖ DC/ 10 9 8 7 6 5 4 3 2 1

CONTENTS

To Marshal and Emma, two of the brightest smiles on the face of my world; thank you, Sarena and Jacob

Special thanks to:

My agent, David Robie, whose professionalism, knowledge, and friendship are appreciated greatly.

The outstanding people at Zondervan, including Tim, Bob, Jack, Jamie, and so many others who personify what makes a good publisher great.

Jim McClellan, whose support and assistance have contributed significantly to my writing success, and whose friendship remains a treasure (even though he's a Buckeye fan).

Kevin Shirk, Esq., one of the world's greatest thinkers and counselors, who has probably forgotten that he encouraged me to complete this book.

Randy and Karla Giminez, two remarkable people who have served me not only as close friends, but as honest "sounding-boards" for my best (and worst!) ideas.

My mom, Pat, who still makes the world's greatest potato salad and apple pie.

And as always, to my wife and foremost fan, Cathy, who remains the best part of me by any measure. Whenever I smile, I'm either working on the next joke or thinking of you.

INTRODUCTION

Hello, and welcome to **Zondervan's Great Bible Trivia Workout,** where you build "brain mass" while toning your Methuselah muscles. (They're the oldest muscles in your body.)

Here, your knowledge of Old and New Testament people, places, and things will shape up, as you laugh, ponder, and enjoy! As your personal "temple trainer," I'll put you through your paces, including:

Matching: Husbands and wives, people and towns, and more.

True/false: Nothing like having a 50–50 chance!

Arrange/correct the story: You be the hero!

Fill in the blank: Challenging, but I have faith in you!

Parts of the story: Isn't it amazing what we can forget?!

And of course, my trademark "multiple guess" (I mean, multiple choice), along with Top Ten Lists, jokes, cartoons, and everything you'd expect from an entertaining and ambitious Bible Trivia challenge bearing the Zondervan name. Oh, I probably should mention there might be a few surprises as well.

In case you're wondering, all Scripture references are found in the **New International Version** of the Bible. It's an outstanding translation, and if you're not using it, well . . . you're part of a shrinking minority. So get one if you don't have one already—you'll thank me later!

Now, the workout stands before us . . . thanks for coming along. Grab that duffel bag and let's head for the gym!

PUTTIN' ON THE SWEATS

PIOUS PAIRINGS:
Matches Made in Heaven (or Possibly Israel)

Pair the following spouses with their respective mates:

___1. Abraham

___2. Paul

___3. Ruth

___4. Joseph

___5. Moses

___6. Lamech (Cain's grandson)

___7. Sapphira

___8. Noah

___9. Jacob

___10. Herodias

___11. Priscilla

___12. Cuza

___13. Gomer

___14. Fred

A. Ananias

B. Joanna

C. Leah

D. No spouse mentioned

E. Wilma

F. Hosea

G. Zipporah

H. Mary

I. Boaz

J. Adah

K. Name unknown

L. Sarah

M. Aquila

N. Herod the tetrarch

(For extra credit, name at least fifty of Solomon's wives and/or concubines.)

Now see if your answers "pair up" with the ones on page 38.

JUST THE FACTS, MA'AM! (OR SIR!)

Which of these were part of Matthew's account of Jesus' birth and early childhood?
(Y = yes; N = no—I like to keep things as simple as possible!)

____1. Magi from the east follow a star

____2. An angel of the Lord appears to Mary in a dream

____3. A decree from Pontius Pilate

____4. A trip to Egypt

____5. A visit from John the Baptist

____6. Joseph's plan to divorce Mary

____7. The angel Gabriel's visit with Mary

____8. A manger in Bethle-hem, and shepherds who search for it

____9. The circumcision of the baby Jesus

____10. Joseph's abstinence from sexual relations with Mary until after Jesus is born

____11. Herod's interest in Jesus' whereabouts

____12. The killing of all male children in Bethlehem aged two and under

____13. An edict by Caesar Augustus requiring a census

____14. The Christ Child's blessing in the temple by Simeon

____15. A problem with Blue Cross of Bethlehem, which claimed it wanted maternity benefits to remain "stable"

Here's a fact that requires less thinking: answers are on page 38.

MIRACLE MATCH

Ready? Let's begin with some Bible miracles. Match the act with the person(s) responsible.

_____ 1. Bitten by a poisonous viper with no ill effect

_____ 2. Led the people across a temporarily divided Jordan River

_____ 3. Produced water from a rock

_____ 4. Made the head of an ax float in the Jordan River

_____ 5. Turned water into wine

_____ 6. His donkey spoke to him

_____ 7. He died after lying about proceeds from a sale

_____ 8. He was fed by ravens

_____ 9. He was rescued from prison by an angel of the Lord

_____ 10. This idol could not survive when placed next to the Ark of the Covenant

_____ 11. Jesus raised him from the dead (he had "crashed" permanently!)

_____ 12. He killed a lion!

_____ 13. Almonds grew on his staff. (Though he preferred "plain.")

_____ 14. Turned computer software into a multi-billion-dollar empire

A. Elijah

B. Lazarus

C. Bill Gates

D. Moses

E. Peter

F. Aaron

G. Balaam

H. Jesus

I. Paul

J. Samson

K. Dagon

L. Ananias

M. Joshua

N. Elisha

Smaller miracle: the answers appear on page 39.

TOTAL RECALL

(Hey, at least it's not your CAR that's being recalled!)
Do your very, very best to fill in the blank with the correct answer. We're going to try one interesting fact from each book of the Bible in succession. Good luck!

1. Noah's ark landed on the mountains of _____.

2. When the Israelites grew tired of waiting for Moses to return from Mt. Sinai, they melted their gold earrings into an idol in the form of a _____.

3. Aaron's sons, Nadab and Abihu, were destroyed for making an improper offering of _____.

4. When the Israelites complained about not having meat, God eventually sent _____ (along with a great plague).

5. God commanded Moses to utterly destroy all of the _____ nations in the "promised land."

6. When Joshua sent spies to scout Jericho, they were aided by a prostitute named _____.

7. _____, a prophetess who judged Israel, instructed Barak to do battle with the Canaanites, and accompanied him.

8. Ruth told Naomi, "Where you go I will go." Naomi was Ruth's _____ .

9. God told Samuel that he was grieved that he had made _____ king of Israel.

10. After David's sins of adultery and murder, the prophet _____ came to tell David of God's impending judgment.

11. When King David was dying, he told Solomon, "Do not let his gray head go down to the grave in peace." He was referring to _____. (Get this and I'm impressed!)

12. The prophet Isaiah told King _____ that the Babylonians would eventually carry off all the wealth stored up by his fathers.

13. Saul's death was ultimately caused by _____.

14. "The report I heard in my own country about your achievements and your wisdom is true. But I did not believe what they said until I came and saw with my own eyes." This was said to King Solomon by _____.

15. While the Israelites were in captivity, _____ issued a decree that the temple of Jerusalem should be rebuilt.

16. When Nehemiah was attempting to rebuild the walls of Jerusalem, one of his detractors said that if as much as a _____ ran across the wall, it would break down.

17. Because of Mordecai and Esther's righteousness and courage, the Jews survived Haman's plot to destroy them. The celebration that commemorates their victory is known as the Feast of _____.

18. Job's three friends came to visit him, but when they saw how great his grief was, no one spoke for _____ days.

19. Psalms is a collection of _____ (how many?) songs.

20. Proverbs says that it is better to have _____ than great riches.

21. The Teacher of Ecclesiastes says that "Everything is _____."

22. The woman in Song of Solomon is referred to as the _____.

23. In chapters 46 and 47, Isaiah predicts the destruction of this empire and its idols. It is _____.

24. God told the prophet Jeremiah not to _____.

25. Ezekiel was instructed by God not to grieve after _____.

26. By interpreting the dreams of King _____, Daniel achieved rank and power in Babylon.

27. Hosea married Gomer, who was a _____, because God told him to.

28. When Joel asked the elders if "anything like this" had ever happened in their days, he was referring to a _____.

29. According to the book of Amos, his prophecies came two years before a significant _____.

30. Obadiah, the shortest book of the Old Testament, is a judgment against the land of _____.

31. The men on the ship on which Jonah was a passenger decided by _____ (what process?) that he was the cause of the tempest.

32. The only element that was capable of killing Superman was _____.

33. Micah says that the country of _____ will be left "a heap of rubble, a place for planting vineyards."

34. Nahum predicts the fall of _____, the capital of Assyria, where Jonah preached more than a century earlier.

35. Habakkuk is concerned that although Judah is guilty of sinful behavior, justice would not be served if they were conquered by the _____, who were even more evil.

36. Zephaniah referred to Jerusalem's officials as roaring lions, and her rulers as evening _____.

37. Haggai questioned the people about living in "paneled houses" while the _____ remained in ruins.

38. Zechariah's third vision involved a man with a measuring line, who told Zechariah that he was going to measure _____.

39. Through Malachi, God says the people have corrupted his covenant with _____.

40. _____ asked Jesus, "Are you the one who was to come, or should we expect someone else?"

41. After Jesus walked on water and got into the boat with his disciples, they crossed and landed at _____.

42. Buzz Lightyear's favorite saying is, "To infinity . . . and _____!"

43. In the parable of the Lost Son, after wasting all of his money, the young man goes into the fields to _____ _____.

44. When Jesus went to Jerusalem for the Jewish _____, he drove the vendors and moneychangers out of the temple.

45. While Stephen was being stoned to death for preaching about Jesus, the witnesses laid their clothes at the feet of a young man named _____.

46. Paul tells the Romans that everyone should submit himself to the _____.

47. Paul told the Corinthian believers, "I planted the seed, _____ watered it, but God made it grow."

48. Paul tells the Corinthians that they should not be "yoked together with _____."

49. The Galatians are instructed to "not become weary in _____ _____ ."

50. The final article in the "full armor of God" is the "_____ of the Spirit, which is the word of God."

51. Paul told the Philippian believers, "For to me, to live is Christ and to die is _____."

52. Paul warns the Colossian believers about the fallacy of worshiping _____.

53. Although Paul and Timothy wanted to return to their friends at Thessalonica, they were hindered by _____.

54. The second letter to the Thessalonians admonishes the people that "If a man will not work, he shall not _____."

55. Yogi the Bear can sleep 'til noon, but before it's dark, he'll have every picnic basket that's in _____ _____.

56. In order for a widow to be supported by the church, she should be at least _____ years old.

57. Timothy's mother is a lady named _____. (Extra credit if you know Timothy's grandmother's name, too.)

58. Titus had been left by Paul to lead the church on the island of _____.

59. Philemon had been the owner of a slave named _____.

60. The author of Hebrews reiterates how Abraham gave a tithe to _____, the king of Salem and priest of God Most High.

61. James compares the _____ to "a fire, a world of evil."

62. Peter says that the wife's role in a marriage is to be _____.

63. Second Peter (First Peter's identical twin brother) reminds us that with the Lord a day is like a _____ years.

64. First John tells his readers that "this is the last hour . . . and the _____ is coming."

65. In the Broadway hit **Fiddler on the Roof**, the instrument played by the fiddler was the _____. (This is NOT a trick question. It is what we call a "gimme". If you get it wrong you may want to consider going back to comic books as your primary source of literature.)

66. Second John is addressed to the "chosen _____", which may be a reference to a specific person or church.

67. John says in book three that _____ (who?) is well spoken of by everyone.

68. Jude identifies himself as "a servant of Jesus Christ and a brother of _____."

69. Between the opening of the sixth and seventh seals, the apostle John saw an angel preparing to put a seal on the foreheads of _____ (number?) Israelites.

70. After taking this "Total Recall" challenge, I need to
_____. (Fill this in according to your own feelings
at this time.) Some options might be:

- grab a snack
- say a quick prayer
- take a long vacation
- get some counseling
- stick with "Wheel of Fortune"
- enter a monastery

Congratulations on finishing. Recall questions tend to be the most challenging, and while I realize you're pretty brilliant—you will discover how much so by checking out the answers on page 40.

So pat yourself on the back, take a deep breath, and let's head on to . . .

CORRECTION, PLEASE!

There seems to be a problem with this version of Solomon's "time for every purpose" soliloquy found in Ecclesiastes 3:1–8. I tried to write it strictly from memory, but I guess my memory ain't what it used to be! See if you can make the necessary corrections **before** you look it up!

(Hint: You may want to **start** by marking each statement that doesn't belong.)

There is a time for everything, and a season for every activity under the sun:

a time to be born and a time to die,

a time to walk and a time to run,

a time to kill and a time to heal,

a time to tear down and a time to build,

a time to pray and a time to refrain from praying,

a time to scatter stones and a time to gather them,

a time to get your driver's license and a time to sign up for Social Security,

a time to gain and a time to lose,

a time to tear and a time to mend,

a time to be silent and a time to speak,

a time to tend the vineyard and a time to drink the wine,

a time to water the flocks and a time to slaughter the lambs,

a time to love and a time to hate,

a time for war and a time for peace,

a time to work and a time to read another Bible trivia book,

a time to share a lime with a mime and a time in your prime when you would climb in grime for a dime.

As I said, I have some real doubts about the accuracy of this. Are you finished with your corrections? Okay, let's turn to page 42 and see what the real version says.

Now it must be time for . . . the very first Top Ten List! (Trumpet fanfare.)

TOP TEN THINGS THE CHILDREN OF ISRAEL RESENTED ABOUT MOSES

10. Could never summon up Coney dogs
9. Discovered that he really meant "skimmed" milk and "ant" honey
8. Could part the sea with his staff, but couldn't part his hair with a comb
7. His tri-level tent
6. Got tired of seeing him wear a T-shirt that said "Pharaoh bites"
5. When he set up a tollbooth halfway across the Red Sea
4. Stoning people for failing to floss
3. Finding out that the supposed "dove sacrifices" he was releasing to the Lord were actually homing pigeons, which returned later when no one was around
2. Threatening to have Aaron's rod turn into Barney the Dinosaur
1. Every time they had a picnic, Moses always let a cloud show up

LOOKS TO ME LIKE YOU'VE GOT
A STAFF INFECTION, MOSES.

SAYS WHO? (GENESIS)

The following multiple guess (rats! I keep saying that! I mean multiple CHOICE) questions are all quotes taken from the book of Genesis. Your job is simply to name the speaker. For instance, if the quote was:

1. "Give me liberty or give me death!" and the choices were:

   A. Harry Truman
   B. Patrick Henry
   C. Daniel Boone
   D. Pat Boone
   E. Garth Brooks

Then you, of course, would answer E, Garth Brooks. Of course, you would be WRONG, because the real answer is D, Pat Boone. But that really isn't important right now, so let's get back to Genesis.

1. "My lords, please turn aside to your servant's house. You can wash your feet and spend the night and then go on your way early in the morning."

   A. Abraham
   B. Joseph
   C. Cain
   D. Lot
   E. Judas

2. "Where is your brother Abel?"

   A. Eve
   B. The serpent
   C. The Lord
   D. Adam
   E. Someone from Publisher's Clearinghouse

3. "Can we find anyone like this man, one in whom is the spirit of God?"

    A. Pharaoh
    B. Joseph
    C. Jacob
    D. Noah
    E. Ruth

4. "I did not laugh."

    A. Lot's wife
    B. Jacob
    C. Abraham
    D. Sarah
    E. Someone who read my first Top Ten list

5. "What if the woman is unwilling to come back with me to this land?"

    A. Lot
    B. Abraham's servant
    C. An angel of the Lord
    D. Isaac
    E. Abraham

6. "I never expected to see your face again, and now God has allowed me to see your children too!"

    A. Rachel
    B. Jacob (also called "Israel")
    C. Leah
    D. Joseph
    E. Someone who bumped into the headless horseman, who was taking his kids on a picnic

7. "Why are you angry? Why is your face downcast?"

   A. The Lord
   B. Noah's wife
   C. Esau
   D. Abel
   E. Mike Tyson's boxing coach

8. "My son, let the curse fall on me. Just do what I say; go and get them for me."

   A. Jacob
   B. Isaac
   C. Leah
   D. Rebekah
   E. Job

9. "Cursed be Canaan! The lowest of slaves will he be to his brothers."

   A. God
   B. Abraham
   C. Noah
   D. Nimrod
   E. Dr. Laura

10. "Come, let us build ourselves a city, with a tower that reaches to the heavens."

   A. "they" (the eastward moving people in the ancient world)
   B. "the Amorites"
   C. "Nimrod, and the renowned men of old"
   D. the tribe of Dan
   E. the Skeetabites (they had been itchin' to build a city for a long time)

11. "Look, this Hebrew has been brought to us to make sport of us!"

    A. Pharaoh's bodyguard
    B. Potiphar's servant
    C. Potiphar's wife
    D. Some men of Sodom
    E. A mockingbird (Hey, if you can dish it out, you'd better be able to take it!)

12. "What have you done to us? How have I wronged you that you have brought such great guilt upon me and my kingdom?"

    A. Amraphel, king of Shinar
    B. Chedorlaomer, king of Elam
    C. Birsha, king of Gomorrah
    D. Abimelech, king of Gerar
    E. James Brown, godfather of soul

13. "For God knows that when you eat of it your eyes will be opened, and you will be like God, knowing good and evil."

    A. The angel who guarded the gates of Eden
    B. Adam
    C. The serpent
    D. Eve
    E. The omniscient narrator

14. "Why have you come to me, since you were hostile to me and sent me away?"

    A. Cain
    B. Isaac
    C. Esau
    D. Joseph
    E. The elephant man

15. "How happy I am! The women will call me happy."

    A. Rachel
    B. Leah
    C. Eve
    D. Bilhah
    E. Happy Gilmore

16. "If you prick us, do we not bleed? If you tickle us, do we not laugh? If you poison us, do we not die?"

    A. Lady Macbeth
    B. The ghost of Hamlet's father
    C. Shylock
    D. King Lear
    E. One of the aliens from "The X Files"

Since I'm apparently starting to digress back (or forward) to Shakespeare, perhaps that means it's time to button this up.

So—if you're satisfied with your choices, turn to page 43 and find out who said what!

OUCH! (PART ONE)—PAINFUL (AND/OR UNUSUAL) WAYS TO DIE

Match the person with his or her respective demise. (The author takes no responsibility for the unfortunate fates of the persons involved in these incidents. He only recommends that you avoid doing this section over lunch!)

____ 1. Had a tent peg driven through his head

____ 2. Died in childbirth while traveling

____ 3. Buried alive

____ 4. Struck by an angel and eaten by worms

____ 5. Trampled to death by a "stampede" of his peers

____ 6. Hit by a piece of millstone thrown from a wall

____ 7. Intentionally set palace on fire, then burned with it

____ 8. Died when a great wind blew down the house

____ 9. Killed by large hailstones

____ 10. Overdosed on sleeping pills

____ 11. Boiled and eaten

____ 12. Beheaded

____ 13. Hanged himself

____ 14. Turned into a pillar of salt

____ 15. Struck dead by God for touching the ark of God

A. Korah and his men

B. Judas

C. Uzzah

D. Rachel

E. Samaritan woman's son

F. Zimri

G. Sheba son of Bicri

H. a royal officer

I. Herod

J. Lot's wife

K. Sisera

L. Job's sons and daughters

M. The Amorites and their allies

N. Abimelech

O. Marilyn Monroe

Wow, are we glad that's over! Hopefully, you were able to use the process of elimination to help you obtain most of the correct answers. On second thought, the process of elimination was used on **all of these people!** Aren't you glad you're **you** and not **them?!**

Need to double check anything before turning to the answers? Go ahead, I'll wait right here. (I'll be humming the Jeopardy theme song while you're rechecking.)

Time's up! Head for page 44, and let's try not to make this too painful.

JEEPERS, CREEPERS, WHAT HAPPENED TO THOSE PEEPERS?!

All of the following are associated with "eye" issues noted in the Bible. See how many you can name!

1. _____ was without sight for three days, then "something like scales" fell from his eyes. (Note: I think they were like **fish** scales rather than **bathroom** scales.)

2. In _____'s vision of the cherubim and wheels, he noted they were full of eyes!

3. After _____ was forced to watch the murder of his sons, his eyes were gouged out.

4. A pair of angels struck a large group of men blind in the evil town of _____.

5. When Jesus first touched this blind man's eyes, he reported that men looked like _____. Jesus touched his eyes a second time and he could see clearly.

6. _____ was 98 years old, and Samuel says "his eyes were so dim that he could not see."

7. _____ was blinded by his captors after his "ladyfriend" aided in a conspiracy against him.

8. When the prophet _____ prayed, God responded by striking the entire army of the king of Aram with blindness.

9. _____, a blind beggar, was healed by Jesus when he came to Jericho.

10. "Then will the eyes of the blind be opened and the ears of the deaf unstopped." This is a quote from the prophet _____.

11. Although _____ has been blind since birth, it's never stopped him from doing the greatest rendition of "Georgia on My Mind" that you'll ever hear.

In the words of the guys from #3 and #7 above, "I'll keep an eye out for ya'!" In the meantime, turn to page 44 for the correct responses to Jeepers, Creepers!

After all of this "Ouch" and "Peepers" stuff, I think it's definitely time to lighten up. Here's another Top Ten list:

TOP TEN THINGS ADAM NEVER WORRIED ABOUT

10. Mother's Day
9. The IRS
8. Eve's old boyfriends
7. Getting a promotion
6. His kids being spoiled by their grandparents
5. Where he put his baby pictures
4. His GPA
3. Missing his immunizations
2. Saving for retirement
1. Faulty genes

And now ladies and gentlemen, to close out chapter one, here's Zacchaeus (Luke 19:1–10), our favorite "stand-up" comic, with a few words:

"Okay, so I'm a stand-up comic who looks like he's sitting down. Hey, I can't help it that I'm short—my father was only a Shuhite! (rim shot) So you're probably wondering why I didn't ask Jesus to make me taller. Actually, I did. And he did. But he didn't add any bulk, so I ended up looking like Gumby. I decided being short wasn't so bad after all.

"Anyway, short people run in our family . . . it was either run or get beat up a lot!

"You've been a great audience! Good luck, and I'll see you at the end of the next chapter."

Pious Pairings
Pages 11-12

1. L. Sarah (Sarai) (Gen. 11)
2. D. No spouse mentioned
3. I. Boaz (Ruth 4)
4. H. Mary (Matt. 1)
5. G. Zipporah (Exod. 2)
6. J. Adah (Gen. 4)
7. A. Ananias (Acts 5)
8. K. Name unknown (Popular legends, however, tend to favor Noah's wife's name being "Anita." Often, Noah was heard to say things like: "Anita hammer!" or "Anita bucket of pitch!" or "Anita 'nother animal to match this one!")
9. C. Leah (Gen. 29)
10. N. Herod the tetrarch (Matt. 14)
11. M. Aquila (Acts 18)
12. B. Joanna (Luke 8)
13. F. Hosea (Hos. 1)
14. E. Wilma (Hanna Barbara—Wow, they're a page right out of history!)

Just the Facts, Ma'am!
Page 13

1. Yes (Matt. 2:1–12)
2. No, the angel appeared to Joseph (Matt. 1:20)
3. No, he didn't appear until Jesus' trial many years later (Matt. 27:1–2, 11–26)
4. Yes (Matt. 2:13–15)
5. No, but Mary did visit John the Baptist's mother and father before the boys were born (Luke 1:39–56)
6. Yes (Matt. 1:19)
7. No (Luke 1:26–38, not Matthew!)
8. No (Luke 2:7–17)
9. No (Luke 2:21)
10. Yes (Matt. 1:25)
11. Yes (Matt. 2:7–8)

12. Yes (Matt. 2:16)
13. No (Luke 2:1)
14. No (Luke 2:25–35)
15. ?? While theologians still debate this at seminary, we do have some facts which were recently unearthed at an archeological dig that I was privileged to attend near Terre Haute, Indiana. The "Hoosier Scrolls" indicate that Mary was a member of an HMO (Holy Mother Organization), which had strict rules:
    1. No patient was to spend more than three days in a manger.
    2. Generic swaddling clothes were to be used at all times. If designer swaddling clothes were requested, the additional cost was the patient's responsibility.
    3. Animals were allowed in the delivery room, but they were forbidden from videotaping the birth.
    4. Payment was made only for the cost of staying in a "ward" (also known as the "barn"). Private "suites" (also known as "stalls") were the patient's responsibility.

Miracle Match
Pages 14-15

1. I. Paul (Acts 28)
2. M. Joshua (Josh. 3)
3. D. Moses (Exod. 17)
4. N. Elisha (2 Kings 6)
5. H. Jesus (John 2)
6. G. Balaam (Num. 22)
7. L. Ananias (Acts 5)
8. A. Elijah (1 Kings 17)
9. E. Peter (Acts 12)
10. K. Dagon (1 Sam. 5)
11. B. Lazarus (John 11)
12. J. Samson (Judg. 14)
13. F. Aaron (Num. 17)
14. C. Bill Gates (MS DOS 6.1)

Total Recall
Pages 16-23

1. Ararat (Gen. 8:4)
2. calf (Exod. 32:4)
3. fire (Lev. 10:1–2)
4. quail (the bird, not Dan) (Num. 11:31–34)
5. nations (Deut. 7:1)
6. Rahab (Josh. 2:1)
7. Deborah (Judg. 4:4–16)
8. mother-in-law (Ruth 1:3–16)
9. Saul (1 Sam. 15:10–11)
10. Nathan (2 Sam. 12:1–13)
11. Joab son of Zeruiah (c'mon, everybody knows that!) (1 Kings 2:5–6)
12. Hezekiah (2 Kings 20:14–19)
13. Saul intentionally falling on his own sword (1 Chron. 10:4)
14. the Queen of Sheba (2 Chron. 9:5–6)
15. Cyrus King of Persia (Ezra 1:1–4)
16. fox (the animal, not Mulder, OR an attractive female) (Neh. 4:3)
17. Purim (Esther 9:26)
    (Author's note: My wife and I had the unique opportunity to visit a Jewish temple when they were celebrating this holiday. It was a special experience that we thoroughly enjoyed and will not forget.)
18. seven (Job 2:13)
19. 150 (Pss. 1–150)
20. a good name (Prov. 22:1)
21. meaningless (Eccles. 1:2)
22. Shulammite (Song of Sol. 6:13)
23. Babylon (Isa. 46–47)
24. marry (Jer. 16:1–2)
25. his wife's death (Ezek. 24:15–18)
26. Nebuchadnezzar (Dan. 2:46–49)
27. adulterous wife (Hos. 1:2)
28. locust attack (and we thought Japanese beetles were a pain!) (Joel 1:2–4)
29. earthquake (Amos 1:1)

30. Edom (Obad. 1:1)
31. casting lots (Jon. 1:7)
32. green kryptonite (Remember? And the red stuff had unpredictable results. Once, it made Superman consider becoming a humor writer! Nasty stuff, that red kryptonite!)
33. Samaria (Mic. 1:6)
34. Nineveh (Nah. 1:1)
35. Babylonians (Hab. 1:6–17)
36. wolves (Zeph. 3:3)
37. Lord's house (Hag. 1:2–4)
38. Jerusalem (Zech. 2:1–2)
39. Levi (Mal. 2:4–8)
40. the disciples of John the Baptist (Matt. 11:2–3)
41. Gennesaret (Mark 6:53)
42. beyond (Toy Story, Disney)
43. feed pigs (Luke 15:15)
44. Passover (John 2:13–16)
45. Saul (Acts 7:58)
46. governing authorities (Rom. 13:1)
47. Apollos (1 Cor. 3:6)
48. unbelievers (2 Cor. 6:14)
49. doing good (Gal. 6:9)
50. sword (Eph. 6:17)
51. gain (Phil. 1:21)
52. angels (Col. 2:18)
53. Satan (1 Thess. 2:18)
54. eat (2 Thess. 3:10)
55. Jellystone Park (Cartoon theme song. Trust me on this one!)
56. sixty (1 Tim. 5:9; of course, they still got senior citizen discounts beginning at age fifty.)
57. Eunice (grandmother: Lois) (2 Tim. 1:5)
58. Crete (Titus 1:5)
59. Onesimus (Philem. 10)
60. Melchizedek (Heb. 7:1–2)
61. tongue (James 3:6)
62. submissive (1 Pet. 3:1) (My how things change!)

63. thousand (2 Pet. 3:8)
64. antichrist (1 John 2:18)
65. oboe (ha ha ha!! Just kidding! If it wasn't a fiddle, we're all in big trouble. But just in case you missed this, here's another opportunity: What color is an orange?)
66. lady (2 John 1:1)
67. Demetrius (3 John 12)
68. James (Jude 1)
69. 144,000 (Rev. 7:4)

Correction Please
Pages 24-25

As I said, I have some real doubts about the accuracy of this. Are you finished with your corrections? Okay, let's see what the real version says:

1. "Under the sun" should actually be "under heaven." (Okay, so I'm being too picky. No point deduction for this!)

The accurate statements I included in my version were:

a time to be born and a time to
    die,
a time to kill and a time to heal,
a time to tear down and a time
    to build,
a time to scatter stones and a
    time to gather them,
a time to gain and a time to lose,
a time to tear and a time to
    mend,
a time to be silent and a time to
    speak,
a time to love and a time to hate,
a time for war and a time for
    peace.

Apparently, I did miss a few! Solomon refuses to take credit (or blame) for the following:

> a time to walk and a time to run,
> a time to pray and a time to
>   refrain from praying,
> a time to get your driver's license
>   and a time to sign up for
>   Social Security (I have a feeling
>   that Solomon was one of the
>   few people of his day who
>   actually HAD social security!),
> a time to tend the vineyard and a
>   time to drink the wine,
> a time to water the flocks and a
>   time to slaughter the lambs,
> a time to work and a time to
>   read another Bible trivia book,
> a time to share a lime with a
>   mime and a time in your
>   prime when you would climb
>   in grime for a dime.

Says Who?
Pages 27-31

1. D. (Gen. 19:1–2)
2. C. (Gen. 4:9)
3. A. (Gen. 41:38)
4. D. (Gen. 18:15)
5. B. (Gen. 24:5)
6. B. (Gen. 48:11)
7. A. (Gen. 4:6)
8. D. (Gen. 27:13)
9. C. (Gen. 9:25)
10. A. (Gen. 11:4)
11. C. Gen. 39:14)
12. D. (Gen. 20:9)

13. C. (Gen. 3:5)
14. B. (Gen. 26:27)
15. B. (Gen. 30:13)
16. C. (Shakespeare's The Merchant of Venice)

Ouch! (Part One)
Pages 32-33

1. K. Sisera (Judg. 4:18–21)
2. D. Rachel (Gen. 35:16–19)
3. A. Korah and his men (Num. 16:31–33)
4. I. Herod (Acts 12:23)
5. H. a royal officer (2 Kings 7:17)
6. N. Abimelech (Judg. 9:52–53)
7. F. Zimri (1 Kings 16:18)
8. L. Job's sons and daughters (Job 1:19)
9. M. The Amorites and their allies (Josh. 10:11)
10. O. Marilyn Monroe (Legend says that Moses once con-
    templated suicide by overdose, but didn't figure he
    could accomplish it with just two tablets.)
11. E. Samaritan woman's son (2 Kings 6:28–29)
12. G. Sheba son of Bicri (2 Sam. 20:22)
13. B. Judas (Matt. 27:5)
14. J. Lot's wife (Gen. 19:26)
15. C. Uzzah (2 Sam. 6:7)

Jeepers Creepers!
Pages 34-35

1. Saul (Acts 9:9,18)
2. Ezekiel (Ezek. 10:9–12)
3. Zedekiah (2 Kings 25:7)
4. Sodom (Gen. 19:11)
5. trees (Mark 8:22–25)
6. Eli (1 Sam. 4:14–15)
7. Samson (Judg. 16:16–21)
8. Elisha (2 Kings 6:18–23)
9. Bartimaeus (Mark 10:46–52)
10. Isaiah (Isa. 35:5)
11. Ray Charles (If you chose Mr. Magoo, you should be completely ashamed of yourself.)

LOW-IMPACT WARM-UP

(Which means I'm concerned that my impact on you has been rather low, but I'm hoping you'll warm up to me pretty soon.)

The Old Testament has some really great stories! One of my favorites is Noah's ark, a saga many of us first heard as kids. Now it's time to find out how much you remember about old Noah and his floating zoo, with this true/false exercise:

WHATEVER FLOATS YER BOAT

____ 1.   Prior to the flood, God is quoted as saying that he is sorry he had made mankind.

____ 2.   God instructed Noah to build the ark with cypress wood and pitch.

____ 3.   The ark was 450 feet long, 75 feet wide, and 25 feet high.

____ 4.   The first person to enter the ark was Noah's father, Methuselah.

____ 5.   God told Noah not to take any food, but rather to slaughter the animals' offspring and eat them.

____ 6.   Noah was to take seven each of every clean animal.

____ 7.   Noah was 600 years old at the time of the flood.

____ 8.   On the ark, along with a wide array of animals and birds, were Noah and his wife, their four sons and their wives.

____ 9.   The waters flooded the earth for 150 days.

____ 10. Scientists who search for Noah's ark are called arkeologists.

_____11. Noah's sons closed the door of the ark after everyone was safely inside.

_____12. The ark eventually came to rest in what are now the Swiss Alps.

_____13. Noah released a dove from the ark, but it returned when it found no dry land.

_____14. The first thing Noah did after vacating the ark was to build a house for his family.

_____15. God promised Noah that he would never flood the earth again, and offered a rainbow as a sign of his new covenant.

I hope all of that information came flooding back to you.

Now it's time to gopher the answers on page 82.

As long as we're already on the subject, I just happen to have a list of the:

TOP TEN LITTLE-KNOWN FACTS
ABOUT THE GREAT FLOOD

10. Only spot of land remaining was Gilligan's Island
9. Noah still managed to wipe out four propellers
8. The Ark actually floated above the Panama Canal
7. The flood allowed various fish schools to study abroad
6. Noah's family wrote the original script for **Waterworld**, then tossed it overboard, hoping it would never be found
5. Deep sea fishing could now be done anywhere
4. Noah's family nicknamed him "Captain Steubing"
3. The Ark was temporarily anchored to the Eiffel Tower, until the last remaining Frenchman insulted Noah and cut the line
2. The elephants kept asking to go for a swim since they all had their trunks
1. Noah's entire family walked funny for the rest of their lives

GETTING YOUR *MASTER'S* DEGREE

(Questions about Jesus from MMLJ—Matthew, Mark, Luke, and John!)

1. When Jesus was twelve, his parents went to celebrate Passover, then left thinking he was with their company. When they discovered him missing, where did they eventually find Jesus?

    A. By the Jordan River with John the Baptist
    B. In the temple, listening to the teachers
    C. With the poor people in the streets
    D. Near the Mount of Olives, praying
    E. With some teenagers, turning vegetables into Reese's Peanut Butter Cups

2. Which of the following correctly reflects Mark's account of the second miraculous feeding of the multitudes?

    A. About four thousand men (and their families) were fed, based on Jesus' blessing of seven loaves of bread and a few small fish
    B. Over nine thousand men, plus women and children, were fed after Jesus blessed two fish and five loaves of bread
    C. The disciples brought ten loaves of bread and eight fish to Jesus, and after blessing it, about one thousand people were fed
    D. Jesus decided against multiplying the fish and bread they had on hand, and instead he ordered pizza for everyone. The miracle was that the pizza arrived on time, still hot, and everyone's order was correct. The people quickly recognized this truly was an act of God!

3. John begins by referring to Jesus as:

    A. The Messiah
    B. The Comforter
    C. The Prince of Peace
    D. The Word
    E. The Lamb

4. According to John's account, whom did Jesus first appear to after his resurrection?

    A. Mary Magdalene
    B. Peter and John
    C. The two Roman guards who were watching the tomb
    D. Joseph of Arimathea
    E. A small crowd of people who were at the cemetery for a Memorial Day service

5. To whom did Jesus say, "Come, follow me, and I will make you fishers of men"?

    A. James and John, the sons of Zebedee
    B. Judas, Mark, and Matthew
    C. Simon Peter and his brother, Andrew
    D. A group of children fishing by the Sea of Galilee
    E. Eddie Fisher, Carrie Fisher, and Bobby Fisher

6. When Jesus said, "I have not found anyone in Israel with such great faith," he was referring to:

    A. Zacchaeus
    B. Peter's mother-in-law
    C. A centurion
    D. A paralyzed man who was let down through the roof
    E. A man who asked Jesus to heal him of his TV football-watching addiction

7. When Jesus came to Nazareth at the outset of his ministry, he went to the synagogue on the Sabbath. From what prophet's book did he read to those gathered there?

   A. Ezekiel
   B. Isaiah
   C. Daniel
   D. Jeremiah
   E. Frankie "Little Prophet" Gambino

8. While they were traveling to Capernaum, Jesus' disciples were arguing about:

   A. What Jesus meant by saying he would "destroy the temple and raise it back up in three days"
   B. Why they had been unable to cast out certain demons
   C. Why Jesus had been so harsh to the Pharisees
   D. Which of them would be the greatest
   E. The best way to fillet Dead Sea salmon

9. According to Luke, Jesus' last words prior to his death on the cross were:

   A. "Father, into your hands I commit my spirit"
   B. "Assuredly, I say to you, today you will be with me in paradise"
   C. "Father, why have you forsaken me?"
   D. "Father, forgive them, for they know not what they do"

10. Why was the woman at Jacob's well surprised that Jesus asked her for a drink?

   A. Because Jews did not associate with Samaritans
   B. Because men never asked women to draw water for them
   C. She realized he knew she was living an immoral lifestyle

D. Because she was a leper, and people generally avoided her
E. Because she could hear the water sloshing in his canteen

11. To whom did Jesus give the nickname "Sons of Thunder"?

A. Andrew and Thomas
B. The Pharisees
C. James and John
D. Matthew and Mark
E. Two puppies he found during a bad storm

12. According to Matthew, the first person to be healed after the Sermon on the Mount was:

A. A woman who had been hemorrhaging for many years
B. A man with leprosy
C. A man with a withered hand
D. A blind man
E. A man who had stumbled and rolled down the mountain

13. When Jesus asked his disciples, "Who do men say that I am?" they responded with all of the following EXCEPT:

A. Jeremiah
B. John the Baptist
C. Elijah
D. Isaiah
E. One of the prophets

14. In the parable of the good Samaritan, which two people passed by the wounded man without helping him?

A. A Pharisee and a scribe
B. A priest and a Levite

C. A scribe and a tax collector
D. A centurion and a Levite
E. Homer and O. J. Simpson

15. Following his resurrection, Jesus appeared to two individuals (one named Cleopas) while they were traveling to:

A. Emmaus
B. Damascus
C. Jerusalem
D. Galilee
E. An Easter dinner

To discover if you've mastered this material, turn to page 82.

YOU ONLY GO AROUND ... TWICE!

All of these people were "brought back" from the dead. See how many you can name.

1. Before bringing the daughter of _____ back to life, Jesus was laughed at by those who heard him say she was "asleep."

2. After Elisha prayed, he warmed this young boy's body with his own. As his life returned to him, the boy sneezed seven times. (We don't know if Elisha said "gesundheit" seven times or not.) The boy is known only as the son of the _____.

3. After falling asleep during one of Paul's messages, _____ fell from a third story loft, only to be revived after Paul fell on him and embraced him.

4. _____ was the brother of Mary and Martha, and had been dead for four days when Jesus commanded him out of the tomb.

5. King Saul disguised himself and visited a medium, who, at his request, raised the spirit of _____.

6. _____ , a woman "who was always doing good and helping the poor," was brought back to life by Peter.

7. According to Luke, Jesus raised a widow's only son from the dead by touching his _____.

8. When the son of the widow with whom he was lodging died, the Old Testament prophet _____ stretched himself out on the young boy three times

and cried out to the Lord. First Kings 17:22 says, "The LORD heard Elijah's cry, and the boy's life returned to him, and he lived."

9. Matthew says that _____ were raised to life and came out of the tombs after Jesus' death on the cross.

10. A dead man thrown in the tomb of _____ came to life after touching the deceased prophet's bones.

Now, my task remains to bring **you** back to life! (You didn't fall asleep on me now, did you? Well, wake up, the answers are on page 83!)

WHERE YA BEEN, STRANGER?

Well, pardner, the trick here is ta match up these here people with the places they tended ta be associated with. Yeah, I know "associated" is a big word fer a cowboy, but I been studyin' vocaberlary. Are ya ready?

____ 1. Samson

____ 2. Ruth & Naomi

____ 3. Magi

____ 4. Hiram

____ 5. Timothy

____ 6. Jonah

____ 7. Lot

____ 8. Batman

____ 9. Esther

____ 10. David

____ 11. Cyrus

____ 12. Moses

____ 13. Isaac

____ 14. Ezekiel

A. The wilderness

B. Gotham City

C. Nineveh

D. Tarsus

E. Sea of Galilee

F. Tyre

G. Philistia

H. Kebar River

I. Bethlehem

J. Honolee

K. Derbe/Lystra

L. Sodom

M. Citadel of Susa

N. Israel

_____15. Simon Peter

_____16. Puff the Magic
        Dragon

_____17. Saul (aka Paul)

O. Gerar

P. Persia

Q. The East

BONUS "MATCHING" QUESTION:

1. The face of the author of this book most closely
    matches that of which Hollywood star?

    A. Brad Pitt
    B. Mel Gibson
    C. A young Robert Redford
    D. "Babe"

The answers are associated with their own home, which is to
your right, on page 83.

As long as ya got yer boots and chaps and bandana on from the last match, ya might as well . . .

MOUNT UP FER A SERMON!

This here is my best recollection of Jesus' "Sermon on the Mount." I bet you pilgrims didn't even know he was ever on a horse, did ya? Yup, in fact Jesus was the only guy I know who could heal his own saddle sores! But before he galloped off to heaven, he left behind some pretty good advice. I gotta warn ya though, this is only what I remember, an' my memory, like the old gray mare, ain't what it used to be. So ya'll just have to decide fer yerself which of these are true an' which ones ain't!!

T = true; A = ain't true

_____ 1. "Blessed are the poor in spirit, for they will inherit the earth."

_____ 2. "Blessed are the peacemakers, for they will be called sons of God."

_____ 3. "Salt that has lost its flavor is only good for feeding to animals."

_____ 4. "Anyone who breaks one of the least of these commandments and teaches others to do the same will be in danger of hell's fire."

_____ 5. "Unless your righteousness surpasses that of the Pharisees and the teachers of the law, you will certainly not enter the kingdom of heaven."

_____ 6. "You're going to put someone's eye out with that thing!"

_____ 7. "Anyone who looks at a woman lustfully has already committed adultery with her in his heart."

_____ 8. "I tell you, Do not resist an evil person. If someone strikes you on the right cheek, turn to him the other also."

_____ 9. "Don't turn away those who would borrow from you, and have mercy on those who steal."

_____10. "When you pray, pray openly in the streets and the synagogues, so that your Father in heaven may reward you openly."

_____11. "When you fast, put oil on your head and wash your face, so that it will not be obvious to men that you are fasting."

_____12. "Where your treasure is, there will your kidneys be also."

_____13. "See how the lilies of the field grow. They do not labor nor spin. Yet I tell you that even the beautiful coat of Joseph was not as lovely as these."

_____14. "Why do you look at the speck of sawdust in your brother's eye and pay no attention to the plank in your own eye?"

_____15. "If you, then, though you are evil, know how to give good gifts to your children, how much more will your Father in heaven give good gifts to those who ask him!"

_____16. "So, in everything, do to others as they do to you; for this sums up the Law and the Prophets."

_____17. "By their fruits you will recognize false prophets. They will sound as sweet as pineapple, but will drive you bananas; their doctrine never compares apples with apples; they want you to think they're just peachy, but in the end it's all sour grapes."

_____18. "A good tree cannot bear bad fruit, and a bad tree cannot bear good fruit."

_____19. "Everyone who has prophesied in my name and cast out demons in my name will surely enter the kingdom of heaven."

_____20. "Those who hear these sayings of mine, and do not put them into practice, will be like a foolish man who built a house and installed cheap windows. Then it rained and the windows leaked, and his wife pitched a fit. Then winter came, and there were awful drafts and his kids all caught colds, and he realized what a stupid decision he had made."

Okay, pardner, it's time to get off yer mount. Let's see jist how much ya did remember 'bout that there sermon! I'm not tryin' to stirrup trouble or anything, but the answer bit is on page 84. WHOA! Don't blame me if you rode down the wrong trail!!

WHAT THE *DEVIL!?*

As you may already have guessed, all of the following have to do with old "what's-his-name."

1. According to 1 Chronicles 21:1, Satan rose up against Israel and incited King David to:

    A. Declare war against the Philistines
    B. Commit adultery with Bathsheba
    C. Murder Saul
    D. Take a census
    E. Enter a "mid-life crisis"

2. With whom did Satan argue regarding the body of Moses?

    A. The angel Gabriel
    B. The archangel Michael
    C. Job
    D. God
    E. The coroner

3. According to the parable of the soils, Satan's purpose is to:

    A. Tempt the sower away from sowing the seed
    B. Take away the word sown in the hearts of the hearers
    C. Distract those by the wayside from hearing the word
    D. Frighten away both sowers and hearers of the word
    E. Provide fertilizer

4. Satan accused God of putting a hedge around this man:

    A. Abraham
    B. Jacob

C. Job

D. Jesus

E. Lot (Every lot should have a hedge around it.)

5. What "devil-incited" act is mentioned by John, directly following the Last Supper?

    A. The upcoming betrayal of Jesus by Judas Iscariot

    B. Peter's three denials of Jesus

    C. The doubts of Thomas

    D. The chief priests' vengeance and plan to arrest Jesus

    E. Judas' diabolical plan to retrieve all of the deposit bottles out of the trash can

6. Paul tells the Corinthians that Satan masquerades as:

    A. "The essence of our desires"

    B. "A thorn in our flesh"

    C. "An unhealing wound of the spirit"

    D. "An angel of light"

    E. "A 1973 Chevy Vega"

7. According to Matthew's Gospel, where was the last place the devil took Jesus when he tempted him?

    A. A very high mountain

    B. On a pinnacle of the temple

    C. The Mount of Olives

    D. The desert

    E. Pizza Hut

8. When the scribes accused Jesus of casting out demons "by the prince of demons," they used this name for Satan:

    A. Baal

    B. Lucifer

    C. Beelzebub

    D. Belial

9. Peter says that the devil walks around like:

    A. "A wise man of old"
    B. "A roaring lion"
    C. "A prince of this world"
    D. "A wolf in sheep's clothing"
    E. "He owns the place"

10. John 8:44 refers to Satan as which TWO of the following?

    A. "A murderer"
    B. "The reaper of death"
    C. "A most vile taskmaster"
    D. "The father of lies"
    E. "Like my brother-in-law"

11. Revelation 20 finds the devil cast into a lake of fire and brimstone with two companions. Who are they?

    A. The beast and the great prostitute
    B. The beast and the false prophet
    C. The great prostitute and the false prophet
    D. The beast and the dark dragon
    E. Butch Cassidy and the Sundance Kid

12. The Bible uses all of these names for Satan except:

    A. Apollyon (when he got really wet, they referred to him as "Apollyon Saturated")
    B. Belial
    C. Abaddon
    D. Molech

Enough "deviltry" for a while. If you're wondering how the devil you did on this, here's the scoop (oops, I mean "pitchfork") on page 84.

As long as we're on the subject, here is a list of the

TOP TEN REASONS SATAN
WAS CAST OUT OF HEAVEN

10. Never used his turn signals
9. Squeezed the toothpaste tube in the middle
8. Did lousy Elvis impersonations
7. Constantly sang the forbidden lyrics to Louie, Louie
6. Inhaled
5. Couldn't part with his eight-track tapes
4. Was teaching an angel choir how to rap
3. Had signed on to endorse Nike's "Just wing it!" campaign
2. Was using his halo as a satellite dish
1. Bit off part of St. Peter's ear in a boxing match

IT'S A LIVING!

Match these Bible personalities with their respective occupations. (Note: Remember the process of elimination. My wife keeps trying this, but she still hasn't figured out how to get rid of **me.**)

____1. Deborah

____2. Abel

____3. Rhoda

____4. Nimrod

____5. Thaddaeus

____6. Obadiah

____7. Barabbas

____8. James son of Zebedee

____9. Haman

___10. Rahab

___11. Tertullus

___12. Luke

___13. Jerry Seinfeld

___14. Lot

___15. Caleb

___16. Aquila

___17. Uriah

___18. Lazarus

A. Cattle herdsman	J. Servant girl
B. Mighty hunter	K. Apostle
C. Doctor	L. Beggar
D. Lawyer	M. Gatekeeper
E. Tentmaker	N. Prostitute
F. Comedian	O. Rebel
G. Keeper of flocks	P. Fisherman
H. Soldier	Q. Spy
I. Prophetess	R. Persian official

You will notice that some jobs haven't changed, while there is an obvious lack of professions such as:

- Web designer
- Insurance adjuster
- Heating and air conditioning specialist
- Flight attendant
- Bioengineer
- Humor writer

In the final analysis, that's probably for the best. Now, for the answers on page 85.

PLAY IT AGAIN, SAMSON!

The story of this "macho-man" is a fascinating one! Which of these statements accurately reflect the biblical account? (true/false)

_____ 1. At the time of Samson's birth, the Israelites were enjoying great prosperity and superiority over their enemies.

_____ 2. An angel had visited Samson's mother prior to her conception, and given her specific instructions about the child.

_____ 3. Samson was an only child at his birth.

_____ 4. Samson's father's name was Samuel.

_____ 5. Samson's mother was forbidden by an angel to drink wine or eat anything unclean during her pregnancy.

_____ 6. Samson's father thought he and his wife were in danger of dying, for "We have seen God."

_____ 7. Samson's first great feat of strength occurred when he was just five years old: He bench-pressed his rather portly Aunt Bessie.

_____ 8. A few days after killing a tiger, Samson discovered a swarm of bees and honey inside its carcass.

_____ 9. Samson killed his first wife when she harassed him about a riddle he proposed to the men at his wedding feast.

_____ 10. Samson burned the fields of the Philistines using three hundred foxes with torches attached to their tails.

_____11. God preserved Samson's life by miraculously providing water.

_____12. While at Gaza, Samson visited a medium to find out how long he would live.

_____13. Delilah agreed to conspire against Samson in return for a large amount of silver.

_____14. Samson told Delilah that he would be unable to free himself if bound with new rope that had never been used.

_____15. Once the Philistines captured Samson, they gouged out his eyes and tied him up outside their temple.

_____16. Samson asked one of the priests to let him lean against the temple's pillars.

_____17. Samson's last recorded words were, "Let me die with the Philistines!"

_____18. Samson killed more Philistines in his final feat of strength than he had killed during his lifetime.

So the Philistine temple turns out to be somewhat of a "pushover" and Samson the ultimate "party crasher."

Now, let's shove on to page 85 for the answers.

SOLOMON SAYS

As the principal contributor to Proverbs, Solomon always gets the credit for them. Actually, there were probably many other "wise guys" involved (I was born too late to get in on it)—guys like Hezekiah, Agur, and Lemuel. They just aren't household names—probably had much smaller harems too!

Select the correct alternative for the following:

1. "The fear of the Lord is _____."

    A. The soul's path to freedom
    B. The beginning of knowledge
    C. A shelter in the time of storm
    D. The gate to salvation
    E. Significantly different than fear itself

2. "_____ calls aloud in the street, she raises her voice in the open squares."

    A. The evil woman
    B. The poor widow
    C. Goodness
    D. Wisdom
    E. The peanut vendor

3. According to Proverbs 2, the immoral woman does all of the following EXCEPT:

    A. Offers intoxicating drink
    B. Left the partner of her youth
    C. Flatters with seductive words
    D. Ignores her covenant with God

4. What THREE criteria must be met before God will "make your path straight"?

    A. Don't lean on your own understanding
    B. Avoid the counsel of fools

C. Acknowledge the Lord in all your ways
D. Trust in the Lord with all your heart
E. Give generously to the Jerry Lewis telethon

5. When it is in your power, do not:

   A. Defraud the God-ordained authority
   B. Allow the devil to gain a foothold
   C. Withhold good from deserving people
   D. Exploit the unfortunate brother
   E. Tee off while the party in front of you is on the green

6. Where does Solomon say one should drink water?

   A. From the river of life
   B. From your own cistern
   C. From Jacob's well
   D. From the perfect streams of knowledge

7. In Proverbs 6, what insect does Solomon direct the lazy man to observe?

   A. The ant
   B. The honey bee
   C. The spider
   D. The butterfly
   E. The cockroach

8. The eighth chapter of Proverbs ends by saying, "All those who hate me love death." **Me** refers to:

   A. The ant
   B. God
   C. Solomon
   D. Wisdom
   E. Oxygen

9. "The mouth of the righteous brings forth wisdom, but a perverse tongue will be _____."

   A. The fool's undoing
   B. Silenced
   C. The devil's tool
   D. Cut out
   E. Pierced

10. A beautiful woman who shows no discretion is like a _____.

   A. Pearl hidden in the mud
   B. Flower blowing in the breeze
   C. Gold ring in a pig's snout
   D. Treasure buried in the sea
   E. Standard sitcom character

11. "There is a way that seems right to a man, but in the end it leads to _____."

   A. Poverty
   B. Death
   C. Humiliation
   D. Ruin
   E. The left

12. Pride goes before destruction. What goes before a fall?

   A. A haughty spirit
   B. The best laid plan
   C. Avarice
   D. Evil
   E. Your balance

13. "_____ is more unyielding than a fortified city."

   A. A simple man
   B. An offended brother
   C. A woman scorned

D. Foolishness

E. Donald Trump

14. *"The glory of young men is their strength, _____ the splendor of the old."*

   A. Accrued wisdom
   B. Their household
   C. A righteous heritage
   D. Gray hair
   E. A good health care plan

15. Proverbs 22:2 says that the rich and the poor have something in common. What?

   A. They will all face God's judgment
   B. They both encounter suffering
   C. The Lord is the Maker of them all
   D. They are all tempted by foolishness and evil
   E. They both despise the middle class

16. *"Do not gloat when _____."*

   A. Your sons call you blessed
   B. Your wealth is greater than your neighbor's
   C. Your enemy falls
   D. The king shows you favor

17. *"A word aptly spoken is like _____ in settings of silver."*

   A. The jewels of Sheba
   B. An emerald of Tyre
   C. Onyx stones
   D. Apples of gold

18. Proverbs 27 encourages the reader to "be sure to know _____."

   A. The condition of your flocks
   B. The intentions of your enemies

C. The state of your soldiers
D. The contents of your storehouse
E. The names of your concubines

19. "A wicked man ruling over a helpless people" is described as being like which TWO of the following:

A. A poisonous serpent
B. A charging bear
C. A hungry leopard
D. A roaring lion
E. A ravenous wolf
F. A napping calico kitten

20. "_____ have no king, yet they advance together in ranks."

A. Ants
B. Locusts
C. Armies
D. Raindrops
E. Marching bands

You should be feeling pretty wise by now! Conquering Proverbs is no small task, but Solomon says you may now look at the answers on page 86.

While we're still on the subject of Solomon, it's common knowledge that this Israelite king was popular with the ladies. In fact, at his peak, he had seven hundred wives of royal birth and three hundred concubines (1 Kings 11:3)!

As a result, he must have had a long list of "opening lines," and probably often utilized some of the

TOP TEN BEST OLD TESTAMENT PICK-UP LINES

10. "Hey, is that a new leaf you're wearing?"
9. "Wanna hear about the time my brothers shoved me down a pit?"
8. "So where were YOU the first two hundred years of my life?"
7. "I'd be happy to show you the sights around Sodom!"
6. "So you're an Amorite? I could've sworn you were a Hittite!"
5. "Wow, an angel!"
4. "I'm just over five hundred, but I can still boogie like a three-hundred-year-old!"
3. "Wow, would you say somebody really burnt an offering?"
2. "This wandering stuff is getting to me. Let's blow this wilderness."
1. "So, what's your favorite commandment?"

And now, once again, our "wee little man" . . . Zacchaeus! (applause)

"Hello ladies and germs, I'm back! I forgot to mention that before I was a tax collector, I was a barber. I quit because I got tired of being referred to as a 'little shaver.' But seriously folks, being short does have some advantages. For instance, it's nice to be able to win a limbo contest without ever having to lean over!

"Hey, you've been a great audience. Now I'm going to turn you over to a good friend of mine, the first person to throw away his 'ship-to-shore' phone when he realized there was no more shore . . . Noah!"

(more applause)

"Thanks, Zak! Cute little fella, that Zacchaeus! It's a good thing he wasn't around during the flood, he would've drowned in the first mud puddle! Do you know why no one played cards on the ark? I was sitting on the deck! (rim shot) But then, I was always a stern guy. Ha ha! I guess it's time to take a bow! Hee hee. Sorry, I guess I went a little overboard! See you at the end of the next chapter!"

LOW-IMPACT WARM-UP ANSWERS

Whatever Floats Yer Boat
Pages 49-50

1. True (Gen. 6:6–7)
2. True (Gen. 6:14)
3. False (Gen. 6:15)
4. False (Gen. 5:26–31) (Methuselah was Noah's grandfather)
5. False (Gen. 6:21)
6. True (Gen. 7:2)
7. True (Gen. 7:6)
8. False (Gen. 7:13)
9. True (Gen. 7:24)
10. False (okay, maybe)
11. False (Gen. 7:16)
12. False (Gen. 8:4)
13. True (Gen. 8:8–9)
14. False (Gen. 8:20)
15. True (Gen. 9:11–17)

Getting Your Master's Degree
Pages 52-56

1. B. (Luke 2:41–50)
2. A. (Mark 8:1–9)
3. D. (John 1:1)
4. A. (John 20:11–18)
5. C. (Matt. 4:18–20)
6. C. (Matt. 8:5–10)
7. B. (Luke 4:16–21)
8. D. (Mark 9:34)
9. A. (Luke 23:46)
10. A. (John 4:9)
11. C. (Mark 3:17)
12. B. (Matt. 8:1–4)
13. D. (Matt. 16:13–17)
14. B. (Luke 10:29–33)
15. A. (Luke 24:13)

You Only Go Around . . . Twice!
Pages 57-58

1. Jairus (Luke 8:41–56)
2. Shunammite woman (2 Kings 4:17–37)
3. Eutychus (Acts 20:9–10)
4. Lazarus (John 11:1–44)
5. Samuel (1 Sam. 28:7–21)
6. Tabitha (also known as Dorcas) (Acts 9:36–41)
7. coffin (Luke 7:11–16)
8. Elijah (1 Kings 17:17–24)
9. "the bodies of many holy people who had died" (Matt. 27:51–53)
10. Elisha (2 Kings 13:20–21)

Where Ya Been, Stranger?
Pages 60-61

1. G. Philistia (Judg. 14:1–4)
2. I. Bethlehem (Ruth 1:1,19)
3. Q. The East (Matt. 2:1)
4. F. Tyre (2 Sam. 5:11)
5. K. Lystra (Acts 16:1)
6. C. Nineveh (Jon. 1:1–2; 3:1–6)
(Note: When people asked Jonah where he was going, he often responded, "Nineveh business.")
7. L. Sodom (Gen. 13:12)
8. B. Gotham City
(Another note: Once Batman and Robin investigated the theft of some Bibles from a Christian bookstore in Gotham City. When they finally found them, Robin opened the boxes and shouted, "Holy Books, Batman!")
9. M. Citadel of Susa (Esther 2:8)
10. N. Israel (2 Sam. 5:1–3)
11. P. Persia (2 Chron. 36:22–23)
12. A. the desert (Num. 32:13)
13. O. Gerar (Gen. 26:6, 17)
14. H. Kebar River (Ezek. 1:1–3)
15. E. Sea of Galilee (Mark 1:16)

16. J. Honolee (Peter, Paul & Mary)
17. D. Tarsus (Acts 22:3)
    Bonus question: A, B, and C are all acceptable.

Mount Up Fer a Sermon!
    Pages 62-64

1. Ain't true (Matt. 5:3, 5)
2. True (Matt. 5:9)
3. Ain't true (Matt. 5:13)
4. Ain't true (Matt. 5:19)
5. True (Matt. 5:20)
6. Ain't true (our moms)
7. True (Matt. 5:28)
8. True (Matt. 5:39)
9. Ain't true (Matt. 5:42)
10. Ain't true (Matt. 6:5–6)
11. True (Matt. 6:17–18)
12. Ain't true (Matt. 6:21)
13. Ain't true (Matt. 6:28–29)
14. True (Matt. 7:3)
15. True (Matt. 7:11)
16. Ain't true (Matt. 7:12)
17. Ain't true (Matt. 7:15–16)
18. True (Matt. 7:18)
19. Ain't true (Matt. 7:21–23)
20. Ain't true (Matt. 7:26–27)

What the Devil!?
Pages 65-67

1. D. (1 Chron. 21:1)
2. B. (Jude 9)
3. B. (Mark 4:15)
4. C. (Job 1:9–10)
5. A. (John 13:2)
6. D. (2 Cor. 11:14)
7. A. (Matt. 4:8)
8. C. (Mark 3:22)
9. B. (1 Pet. 5:8)

10. A, D. (John 8:44)
11. B. (Rev. 20:10)
12. D. (Rev. 9:11; 2 Cor. 6:15)

It's a Living!
Pages 70-71

1. I. (Judg. 4:4)
2. G. (Gen. 4:2)
3. J. (Acts 12:13)
4. B. (Gen. 10:8–9)
5. K. (Matt. 10:3)
6. M. (Neh. 12:25)
7. O. (John 18:40)
8. P. (Matt. 4:21)
9. R. (Esther 3:1)
10. N. (Josh. 2:1)
11. D. (Acts 24:1)
12. C. (Col. 4:14)
13. F.
14. A. (Gen. 13:5–11)
15. Q. (Num. 13:1–6)
16. E. (Acts 18:2–3)
17. H. (2 Sam. 11:6–7)
18. L. (Luke 16:19–31)

Play It Again, Samson!
Pages 72-73

1. False (Judg. 13:1)
2. True (Judg. 13:3–5)
3. True (Judg. 13:2–3)
4. False (Judg. 13:2)
5. True (Judg. 13:14)
6. True (Judg. 13:22)
7. False (Judg. 14:6)
8. False (Judg. 14:8)
9. False (Judg. 15:1–2, 6)
10. True (Judg. 15:4–5)
11. True (Judg. 15:18–19)

12. False (Judg. 16:1)
13. True (Judg. 16:5)
14. True (Judg. 16:11)
15. False (Judg. 16:21)
16. False (Judg. 16:26)
17. True (Judg. 16:30)
18. True (Judg. 16:30)

Solomon Says
Pages 74-78

1. B. (Prov. 1:7)
2. D. (Prov. 1:20)
3. A. (Prov. 2:16–19)
4. A, C, D. (Prov. 3:5–6)
5. C. (Prov. 3:27)
6. B. (Prov. 5:15)
7. A. (Prov. 6:6)
8. D. (Prov. 8:36)
9. D. (Prov. 10:31)
10. C. (Prov. 11:22)
11. B. (Prov. 14:12)
12. A. (Prov. 16:18)
13. B. (Prov. 18:19)
14. D. (Prov. 20:29)
15. C. (Prov. 22:2)
16. C. (Prov. 24:17)
17. D. (Prov. 25:11)
18. A. (Prov. 27:23)
19. B, D. (Prov. 28:15)
20. B. (Prov. 30:27)

3

STARTING TO EXPIRE

Oops! I mean perspire! And there's no easier way to perspire than to turn up the heat! So let's get started with:

FIRE IN THE HOLE!!!

All of the following involve fire. "Match" 'em up!

_____ 1. Two of his sons died when their offering "backfired."

_____ 2. The Lord's fire consumed them for complaining.

_____ 3. His cry to God resulted in fire from heaven consuming a sacrifice, and a defeat for the prophets of Baal.

_____ 4. God provided this leader with a "pillar of fire" so that his people could travel by night.

_____ 5. Their city was destroyed by burning sulfur out of the heavens.

_____ 6. He watched as Elijah was taken up in a "chariot of fire."

_____ 7. An angel spoke to them, then ascended into the flame of a burning sacrifice.

_____ 8. A seraph touched a fiery "live coal" to this prophet's mouth.

_____ 9. They guarded Eden with flaming swords after Adam and Eve were banished at the outskirts of the camp.

_____ 10. While he watched, an angel of the Lord produced fire from a rock, which consumed meat and bread.

_____ 11. In his vision, he saw God on a throne flaming with fire and a river of fire flowing before him.

_____12. This leader's indifference brought his country hail and lightning

_____13. He put Shadrach, Meshach, and Abednego in a fiery furnace when they refused to worship him.

_____14. This New Testament writer compared the tongue to a fire.

_____15. Peter explained the Pentecostal "fire" of the Holy Spirit as an event predicted by this prophet.

_____16. She has dubiously been blamed for starting the Great Chicago Fire of 1871.

A. Nebuchadnezzar

B. Elisha

C. Isaiah

D. Mrs. O'Leary's cow

E. Gideon

F. Aaron

G. Joel

H. Daniel

I. Elijah

J. Some Israelites

K. James

L. Manoah & his wife (Samson's parents)

M. Pharaoh

N. Moses

O. Lot's family

P. Cherubim

Boy, I'm glad that's over—my computer was starting to smoke! Now it's time to find out how hot you did! (Hopefully you're at least getting warm!) Check page 120 for the infernal answers.

Okay, up an' Adam! I mean up an' at 'em! Well, no, I guess I really do mean ADAM! Let's find out how much you know about the Bible's first family. It's

ADAM'S FAMILY

(True/False)

____ 1.   Immediately after creating Adam, God created the cattle and beasts.

____ 2.   Adam was formed from the dust on the ground.

____ 3.   The river that watered Eden eventually became part of the headwaters of the Tigris and Euphrates rivers.

____ 4.   Eve was created while Adam was naming the animals.

____ 5.   The Lord commanded Adam and Eve not to eat of the tree of the knowledge of good and evil.

____ 6.   The serpent warned Eve that eating the forbidden fruit would result in God's wrath.

____ 7.   The first result of Adam and Eve's disobedience was recognition of their nakedness.

____ 8.   Adam named his wife **Eve,** because she had led him into sin.

____ 9.   Part of God's curse on humanity for eating from the forbidden tree was pain in childbirth and difficulty in raising crops.

____ 10.   The last thing God did for Adam and Eve before banishing them from Eden was provide garments for them.

____ 11.   Adam and Eve's family consisted of themselves and two sons named Cain and Abel.

_____12. After God showed favor for Cain's offering instead of his, Abel murdered his brother.

_____13. Even though a murder had been committed, God still provided some protection for the killer.

_____14. Adam and Eve had a grandson named Seth.

_____15. Adam lived well over nine hundred years, but no mention is made regarding Eve's death.

_____16. God's final judgment upon Adam's family was tearing down the tree house Cain and Abel had built in the tree of the knowledge of good and evil.

Well, if you didn't know these people from Adam, it may be that your tree of knowledge hasn't been watered often enough. The apples of wisdom I generally refer to as answers are on page 120.

It's only fitting that we close this quiz with a little music about Adam's family. Use the tune from the old TV show of the same name. Don't forget to put in the ta da da da, snap snap (finger snaps) between verses! Ready?

> *Ta da da da, snap snap*
> *Ta da da da, snap snap*
>
> *God got the world a spinning*
> *And as he sat there grinning,*
> *He decided on beginning*
> *Old Adam's family!*
> *Ta da da da (etc. etc.)*
>
> *From dust he founded Adam,*
> *Whose rib became his madam,*
> *God made 'em and he had 'em,*
> *They're Adam's family.*

In Eden's where he placed 'em,
But a snake and sin disgraced 'em
God thought he ought to waste 'em,
That Adam's family.

One thing led to another,
Then one son killed his brother.
"He gets it from his mother,"
Said Adam emphatically!

Instead of showing unction,
They derailed at the junction.
This model of dysfunction,
They're Adam's family.

And as my song is ended,
If anyone's offended,
Remember we're descended
From Adam's family!

(Tune in next week to find out if Johnny Cochran can get Cain released on his own recognizance.)

IF WE BUILD IT . . . THEY WILL COME!
BUILDING PROJECTS OF THE BIBLE

Warning: From houses to church additions, building projects have been known to result in everything from injuries to divorces to nuclear wars. They are never to be entered into lightly!

See how many of the following biblical construction efforts you can identify.

1. _____ was credited with building the city of Nineveh.

2. In Jesus' parable, the rich man wanted to tear down his _____ and build larger ones.

3. King Solomon spent thirteen years building _____.

4. The men of Reuben, Gad, and the half-tribe of Manasseh built a "great, impressive _____" by the Jordan River in Canaan, which nearly led to a civil war.

5. At Jesus' transfiguration, Peter wanted to build three _____ on the mountain.

6. _____ was forbidden by God to build a temple.

7. Proverbs 9 says that "wisdom has built her _____."

8. Nehemiah's building project was the reconstruction of _____.

9. Jesus metaphorically stated that he could rebuild the _____ in three days.

10. Prior to the construction of _____, the whole earth had one language.

11. The army of Troy built a large wooden _____, then hid inside.

12. The prophet _____ rebuked his people for building nice houses for themselves while the temple still remained a ruins.

13. King _____ fortified Shechem in the hill country of Ephraim. (Get this right without looking it up and you are truly a Bible scholar!)

14. The first great temple of Jerusalem was built under King _____.

15. While on Mt. Sinai, the first thing God instructed Moses to have the people build was _____.

All of this building stuff is starting to make me tired! Of course, listening to my eight track tape of the Carpenters isn't helping any either. Let's turn to page 121 and see if we can nail down the answers.

Of course, there were many sites that were not mentioned for various reasons. So as an added bonus, here is a list of the

TOP TEN "BUILDINGS" NOT FOUND IN THE BIBLE

10. Yankee Stadium
9. The Taj Mahal
8. Trump Towers
7. Mall of America
6. Big Ben
5. The Eiffel Tower
4. 3-Com Park
3. Leaning Tower of Pisa
2. Cinderella's Castle, Disneyland
1. Alcatraz

FALSE GODS PUT IDOL HANDS TO WORK

The following questions involve idols and pagan gods found in the Scriptures. Here is your list from which to choose:

Diana	Dagon	Thor
Chemosh	Anakin	Shushan
A golden calf	Zeus	Billy Idol
Ashtoreth	Ahaz	Micah's idols
Baal	Molech	A "Tickle Me Elmo" idol
Cubit	Venus	Succoth Benoth

(Caution: Although all of the correct answers are here, at least one will be used twice. There may also be a few "extra" things that are from another source, or fabricated by you-know-who! Good luck!)

1. Those who worshiped this god probably also worshiped the moon, sun, and constellations.

    Answer: _____

2. Aaron built an altar before it and said, "Tomorrow there will be a festival to the Lord."

    Answer: _____

3. When the children of Dan rebuilt their city, they set these up as their gods.

    Answer: _____

4. This Philistine idol tipped over while "rooming" with the ark of the covenant.

    Answer: _____

5. This god was associated with fire, and children were sacrificed to him.

    Answer: _____

6. After seeing a lame man healed, certain people of Lystra referred to Barnabas as this god.

   Answer: _____

7. Jephthah the Gileadite acknowledged him as god of the Amorites.

   Answer: _____

8. Solomon eventually worshiped this goddess of the Sidonians.

   Answer: _____

9. This idol sang "Get Outta My Dreams."

   Answer: _____

10. This was a Babylonian god, put in the high places of Samaria.

    Answer: _____

11. The Lord instructed Gideon to remove an altar of this god and a wooden image beside it.

    Answer: _____

12. This king sacrificed his son by fire to a pagan god.

    Answer: _____

13. Neither an idol nor a god, just a great pod-racer!

    Answer: _____

So much for all this idol chatter! Let's get right to the solutions on page 121.

KING, PRIEST, PROPHET, OR JUDGE

Okay, we're going to keep this one real simple. These are your four choices. I give you the names, and you decide which of these "titles" the person held. As always, the Bible provides the last word. Any ties, I win!

Author's note: Occasionally, there may be a rare instance where one of these people actually fit into more than one category. For instance, biblical references for Jesus could actually place him under all four categories (therefore, I'm not including him in the list!). However, if you see two spaces following the name, that means that the Bible is clear that they occupied those two offices. If you're in doubt, go for the answer for which the person would be most noted.

If you find references to back up an answer that does not agree with mine, I'll acquiesce. But just keep in mind that I may do the same thing when I'm reading YOUR book!! Now let's get started already!

1. Samuel
   _____
   _____

2. Deborah
   _____
   _____

3. Ahab
   _____

4. Ananias
   _____

5. Moses
   _____

6. Tola
   _____

7. Aaron
   _____
   _____

8. Saul
   _____

9. Eli
   _____

10. Isaiah
   _____

11. Judy

    _____

12. John the Baptist

    _____

    _____

13. Hezekiah

    _____

14. Hiram

    _____

15. Gideon

    _____

16. Jeshua

    _____

17. Melchizedek

    _____

    _____

18. Samson

    _____

19. Elijah

    _____

20. Nebuchadnezzar

    _____

21. Enoch

    _____

22. Kong

    _____

Now let's see if we can discover . . . THE TRUTH! I prophesy that the answers are on page 122.

Now it's time to . . .

STOP YOUR "WINE-ING"

Yes, as you may have guessed, the upcoming multiple choice questions all have wine as a common element. So ingest the questions slowly and methodically—roll them around in your brain, then say something like:

"Hmmm, these questions seem to make a statement without being presumptuous."

There, now that you've displayed your obvious surfeit of **chic,** see if you can get at least a couple of the correct answers!

1. What did Jesus say would be the result of putting new wine into old wineskins?

   A. The old wineskins would destroy the flavor of the wine
   B. The old wineskins would not allow the new wine to ferment properly
   C. Old wineskins may poison the wine
   D. The old wineskins would burst
   E. You wouldn't get back your ten-cent deposit on the old wineskins

2. Abstaining from wine, vinegar made from wine, and grape juice were all a part of:

   A. God's requirements for Moses
   B. The vow for Nazarites
   C. Paul's suggestions for church deacons
   D. Aaron's sanctification process for Levite priests
   E. A boycott of Mogen David

3. This prophet promised a coming feast for God's people featuring "the finest of wines."

   A. Jeremiah
   B. Isaiah

    C. Daniel

    D. Ezekiel

    E. "Duffy"

4. Joseph interpreted this man's dream, which involved squeezing clusters of grapes, then serving the drink to Pharaoh.

    A. The cupbearer

    B. The baker

    C. The butcher

    D. Potiphar

5. Proverbs 23 states that the last thing red wine does is:

    A. Destroy the drinker

    B. Sting like a scorpion

    C. Poison like a viper

    D. Seduce like a prostitute

    E. Get you arrested for D.U.I.

6. Where was Jesus when he turned water into wine?

    A. The Passover celebration

    B. The Last Supper (in an upper room)

    C. A wedding

    D. A funeral wake

7. Noah's excess with wine, and his youngest son's shameful behavior, resulted in a curse on whose descendents?

    A. Canaan

    B. Ham

    C. Shem

    D. Tubal

8. Paul encouraged him to "use a little wine" for his stomach problems and frequent illnesses.

    A. Luke

    B. Silas

C. Barnabas

D. Timothy

E. Caesar

9. When King Xerxes threw a feast in the citadel of Susa, which of the following best reflects the use of the royal wine?

A. Only the king and his guests of honor could drink it

B. Each guest was allowed to drink in his own way and was served what he wished

C. Refusing the king's wine would be to risk death

D. Only women and eunuchs were prohibited from drinking it

E. There was a cash bar

10. Hosea said that wine and new wine do what?

A. Remove understanding from the people

B. Become the snare of Baal

C. Mock the soul

D. Rage against the spirit

11. Who was accused of being "full of new wine"?

A. The Jews who created a golden calf as an idol, while Moses was on the mountain

B. Paul, when he preached in Athens at the Areopagus

C. The apostles on the day of Pentecost

D. Peter, when he cut off the soldier's ear at Gethsemane

E. The serpent, when he deceived Eve

12. According to Psalm 75, which of the following are true regarding the symbolic wine of the Lord? (Two answers)

A. It is made from the grapes of heaven

B. It is foaming

C. Only the righteous shall taste it

D. It is mixed with spices

E. It shouldn't be served with pork

13. When Jesus and his disciples shared wine at the last supper, he stated that he would not drink it again until:

A. He met with them in the upper room following his resurrection

B. Peter had denied him three times

C. He was finished praying on the Mount of Olives

D. They all met in his Father's kingdom

14. Isaiah invites everyone to come to a place where, without money, you can buy wine and:

A. Milk

B. Bread

C. Cheese

D. Meat

E. Doritos

15. What image from Revelation is associated with wine?

A. The beast

B. The great prostitute

C. The Lamb

D. The false prophet

E. The apostle John's wedding anniversary

16. Who used wine as a disinfectant to help an injured man?

A. Elisha, after a man was injured by an ax head while chopping trees

B. A Samaritan, helping a man who had been beaten and robbed

C. Saul's servant, after Saul was pierced by an arrow

D. Luke, to assist Paul after he was stoned in Lystra

E. David, trying to clean up Goliath's severed head

17. According to Numbers 15, an offering of wine was to be included with all of the following sacrifices EXCEPT:

    A. A lamb or young goat
    B. A young bull
    C. A dove
    D. A ram

18. God told Jeremiah that every _____ was to be filled with wine.

    A. Barrel
    B. Pitcher
    C. Flask
    D. Wineskin
    E. Sailor

I will give no solutions to the questions about wine—before it's time. Okay . . . it's time! Let's toast the answers on page 122.

FARM OUT, MAN!!!

The Bible uses agricultural terms generously and in both literal and figurative ways. So fire up your allegorical tractor, hitch up your symbolic eight-bottom plow, then get real and answer these true/false questions.

_____ 1. Part of the additional details of the law given to Moses, after he had broken the first two tablets, involved a day of rest, even during plowing season and harvest time.

_____ 2. In 2 Corinthians, Paul refers to God as not only the one who supplies seed to the sower, but also gives him bread for food.

_____ 3. Amos talks of locust attacks immediately after the king's plantings.

_____ 4. James criticized the rich for stealing cattle which belonged to poor farmers.

_____ 5. Ruth went to a field belonging to Boaz and worked hard to assist him as his workers planted barley.

_____ 6. Joel's opening chapter discusses agricultural destruction from both locusts and a severe drought.

_____ 7. In Isaiah 5, the prophet compares Israel to God's garden and God's people to flowers.

_____ 8. In his second letter to Timothy, Paul says that the landowner always partakes of the crops before the farmer.

_____9. King David sponsored the first Farm-Aid concert which featured the band "Earth, Wind, Fire, & Brimstone."

_____10. If a man's livestock fed in another man's field, Jewish law required restitution be made from the best of the livestock owner's field and vineyard.

_____11. Paul said that hope of sharing the harvest should be common to both the plower and the thresher.

_____12. Joseph revealed a dream to his brothers, which involved their sheaves of grain bowing down to his.

_____13. Paul told the Corinthians that Jesus Christ had planted seeds that Paul had watered, but that spiritual growth came only through faith.

_____14. Jesus told his disciples that he had sent them to reap what they had not worked for.

_____15. According to Proverbs, a virtuous wife not only buys a field, but also plants a vineyard.

_____16. Jeremiah's cry to "cut off . . . the sower, and the reaper with his sickle at harvest" was part of his announcement of judgment against Persia.

_____17. According to Old Testament law, if a man had planted a vineyard and not yet eaten its fruit, he could be excused from military service.

_____18. According to Haggai, God's anger over the unrestored condition of the temple led to a flood, which destroyed most of the crops raised by the remnant of Jews in Jerusalem.

_____19. Adam's original task in Eden was to work and take care of the garden.

_____20. Jesus said that the smallest seed people plant in the ground is the mustard seed, and the herb that springs up from it is also very small.

_____21. One of John's visions in Revelation involved the great prostitute, who was driving a large John Deere tractor and chasing 144,000 Jews around a bean field.

And now, since I realize you are a reader who is outstanding in your field . . . I'm going to see if I can raise the answers (rather than just another load of fertilizer). Let's plow ahead! Ahead of lettuce and ahead of cabbage, putting all that aside of beef, and combining the correct responses. The "answer barn" is on page 123.

PETER HAS A SECOND PROPHETIC VISION.

Speaking of stock (which I just **was** in case you didn't notice), did you know a fair amount of stocks were for sale in Bible times? To prove my point, let me share a list of the

TOP TEN OLD TESTAMENT STOCKS

10. Idols R Us
9. Judah Online
8. Steerox
7. Exxonodus
6. Chase-Manasseh Bank
5. MicahSoft
4. General Ecclesiastic
3. I.B.M (Israel Barley & Meal)
2. Samsonite
1. Wool Mart

OUR TOWN

Ah, yes . . . home! There's nothing quite like the familiar sights, friendly sounds, and transcendent aromas that welcome us back to those beloved places that house our happiest memories. (Okay, I suppose if there was fire and brimstone involved, all of your memories might **not** be happy.)

Your mission is to choose which of the following cities and towns are described below. Use this list:

Tyre	Endor	Sidon
Bethany	Gomorrah	Nazareth
Rome	Jerusalem	Shiloh
Ai	Gaza	Ephesus
Philippi	Nineveh	Joppa
Damascus	Athens	Hebron
Jericho	Cana	Bethlehem
Antioch	Atlantis	

All of these will be used exactly ONCE. Good luck!

1. Our town probably had its share of mediums and diviners over the years, and one night King Saul came to visit one of them.

   Answer: _____

2. Jesus came to our village to see his friends Mary, Martha, and Lazarus. Once, he even brought Lazarus back from the dead!

   Answer: _____

3. We lived in a rough area; people did nasty things. Our neighborhood was wiped out by fire and brimstone from heaven.

   Answer: _____

4. We had a great little city with thick, high walls, but a local prostitute sold us out and we were conquered by the Israelites.

    Answer: _____

5. While Paul was in our neck of the woods, even his aprons and handkerchiefs carried healing powers. As a result of this, many of our magicians repented and burned their sorcery books.

    Answer: _____

6. Our metropolis was tricked and ambushed by Joshua, and all 12,000 of our inhabitants were slaughtered in one day.

    Answer: _____

7. We were considered the prime city of Macedonia. While here, Paul and Silas were flogged and then tossed into our prison. This event was followed by an earthquake.

    Answer: _____

8. Our town was originally called Ephrath, and we are noted for several things: Rachel was buried here, Ruth and Naomi returned to live here, we are the hometown of King David . . . the list goes on and on!

    Answer: _____

9. My city found Paul encountering many idols on his visit. He spoke to the Epicurean and Stoic philosophers about Christianity.

    Answer: _____

10. We were instrumental in providing materials for Solomon's temple. Our king's servants cut cedar and

cypress trees in Lebanon and floated them down the coast of the Mediterranean Sea.

Answer: _____

11. Peter was in our seacoast hamlet when he had a vision of a great sheet full of animals being lowered from heaven.

Answer: _____

12. Our settlement is probably best known for the cave of Machpelah, where both Sarah and Abraham were laid to rest.

Answer: _____

13. Although our history was one of resisting Israel, Jesus still paid us a visit, and healed a woman's daughter of demon possession.

Answer: _____

14. Our great city was the capital of the Assyrian empire, and is associated with at least one "fishy" story.

Answer: _____

15. Our Syrian town became the home of the first Gentile-populated church.

Answer: _____

16. My city has a fascinating history. It was originally called Salem, but has been referred to as "Zion" and the "Holy City."

Answer: _____

17. We're probably best known for a wedding attended by Jesus, where he performed his first miracle: turning water into wine.

Answer: _____

18. Samson once ripped off our city's main gate (posts and all!) and carried them up a hill!

    Answer: _____

19. Paul met Aquila and Priscilla in Corinth. They were Jews who left my city when Claudius ordered all the Jews to leave.

    Answer: _____

20. While dancing in a celebration, many of our town's daughters were kidnapped to become wives for the men of Benjamin's tribe.

    Answer: _____

21. The disciple Philip was asked by his friend (and soon to be fellow apostle) Nathanael if "anything good" could come out of my village.

    Answer: _____

22. Saul was on his way to our city when he saw a bright light from heaven and was temporarily blinded.

    Answer: _____

23. My city was buried under the Atlantic and people are still trying to find it!

    Answer: _____

If you managed to find your way to all of the right towns and cities, I'd like to take you along on my next vacation! Let's find out how you did! Visit page 124 for the answers.

WHOSE ZOO IN THE BIBLE?

The following questions all relate to animals which appear in the Bible. Admittedly, some of them would probably not be found in a zoo. Of course, if indeed they were in the Bible, they obviously all would be very DEAD by now. And who in their right mind would want to go to a zoo to see a bunch of dead animals?

See if you can name the critters encompassed by the verses below.

(Note: for our purposes, animals may actually be reptiles or rodents. I am also going to give you the Scripture reference with the question, since it may jog your memory in the right direction!)

1. "The infant will play near the hole of the _____ ."
    (Ref: Isa. 11:8)

2. "The king [Solomon] had a fleet of trading ships at sea along with the ships of Hiram. Once every three years it returned, carrying gold, silver and ivory, and _____ and _____." (Ref: 1 Kings 10:22)

3. "'I will turn her [Babylon] into a place for _____ and into swampland; I will sweep her with the broom of destruction,' declares the Lord Almighty."
    (Ref: Isa. 14:23)

4. "The demons begged Jesus, 'If you drive us out, send us into the herd of _____.'" (Matt. 8:31)

5. (Me again! This happens to be another question with two parts, and while that may be obvious, it might be helpful to know that the actual identity of both of these "animals" is unknown.) "Look at the _____, which I made along with you and which feeds on

grass like an ox." "Can you pull in the _____ with a fishhook, or tie down his tongue with a rope?" (Ref: Job 40:15; 41:1)

6. "Babylon . . . will be overthrown by God like Sodom and Gomorrah. She will never be inhabited. . . . But desert creatures will lie there, _____ will fill her houses; there the _____ will dwell, and there the wild _____ will leap about." (Ref: Isa. 13:19–21)

7. "Of the animals that move about on the ground, these are unclean for you: the weasel, the rat, or any kind of great _____." (Ref: Lev. 11:29)

8. "As the _____ pants for streams of water, so my soul pants for You, O God." (Ref: Ps. 42:1)

9. "John's clothes were made of _____'s hair, and he had a leather belt around his waist." (Ref: Matt. 3:4)

10. "Then I saw three evil spirits that looked like like _____; they came out of the mouth of the dragon, out of the mouth of the beast, and out of the mouth of the false prophet." (Ref: Rev. 16:13)

11. "He removed from the entrance to the temple of the Lord the _____ that the kings of Judah had dedicated to the sun." (Ref: 2 Kings 23:11)

12. But he answered and said, "It is not right to take the children's bread and toss it to their _____." (Ref: Matt. 15:26) (Author's Little Insight: This comment took place while Jesus was traveling in the region of Tyre and Sidon. If you've never considered the relationship between these two towns, it's fairly simple: when you start to Tyre, you need to Sidon awhile.)

13. "The beast I saw resembled a _____, but had feet like those of a _____, and a mouth like that of a _____." (Ref: Rev. 13:2)

14. "In that day men will throw away to the _____ and _____, their idols of silver and idols of gold, which they made to worship." (Ref: Isa. 2:20)

15. "The hired hand is not the shepherd who owns the sheep. So when he sees the _____ coming he abandons the sheep and runs away." (Ref: John 10:12)

16. "Many _____ surround me; strong _____ (same animal) of Bashan encircled me. Roaring _____, tearing their prey open their mouths wide against me." (Ref: Ps. 22:12–13)

17. "As I was thinking about this, suddenly a _____ with a prominent horn between his eyes came from the west, crossing the whole earth without touching the ground. . . ." (Ref: Dan. 8:5)

18. "So he (Samson) went out and caught three hundred _____ and tied them tail to tail in pairs. He then fastened a torch to every pair of tails, lit the torches and let (them) loose in the standing grain of the Philistines." (Ref: Judg. 15:4–5)

19. " . . . saying to them 'Go to the village ahead of you, and just as you enter it, you will find a _____ tied there, which no one has ever ridden. Untie it and bring it here.'" (Ref: Mark 11:2)

20. Now that my animal section is finished, I'm going to go take a nap with Barney, my purple, stuffed _____.

ZOO–M to page 124 for the answers.

"Well, hello again! Noah here to welcome you to the end of chapter three. It's only fitting that I get a chance to talk to you right after a quiz about animals. After all, I got to get real 'up close and personal' with a **boatload** of 'em for a good long time, and let me tell you, it was no picnic: giraffes complaining that there wasn't enough headroom, snakes always biting the other animals, parrots always mimicking me, yada yada yada. Looking back, I don't know how we kept from going under!

"Thanks, everybody! You're the best! And now, here's a good friend, and a true 'babe magnet': His Majesty, King Solomon!"

(Thunderous applause, bowing, etc.)
"Thanks, Noah! Boy, I'm sure glad the flood happened in your day instead of mine. I would've had all I could handle just building a boat big enough for all my wives and concubines! Talk about a 'Carnival Cruise!'

"Anyway, Noah, did you hear about the priest who was killed by an arrow in Jerusalem last week?"

"No, Your Highness. Where was he hit?"

"In the temple!" (rim shot)

"Uh, King, how about closing us out with a song?"

"Sure, Noah, I thought you'd never ask!"

My Israeli Girls

(To the tune of "California Girls")

Well, Heshbon girls are sweet,
I like to watch 'em by the pools —
And the Judah dolls who live way down south
Can make the men just act like fools!
The Great Sea girls of Joppa
Have a smile that's sure to please,
And there's sweethearts up in Tyre and Sidon —
I love those female Lebanese!

Chorus:
I wish they all could be my Israeli girls.
(Wish they all could be my Israeli girls.)
Wish they all could be my Israeli girls.
Now Jerusalem's filled with opulence,
The livin' is just fine—
And every gorgeous babe I see
Can be my wife or concubine!
My father David fought a lot,
And I don't know what for,
Cause I've got a better philosophy
I'd rather "make love, not war."

I sure am glad I got my Israeli girls.
(Sure am glad I got my Israeli girls.)
I sure am glad I got my Israeli girls.
Girls, girls, girls, got hundreds of girls . . .
Girls, girls, girls, got thousands of girls . . .
(Repeat and fade)

Fire in the Hole!!!
Pages 88-89

1. F. (Lev. 10:1–2)
2. J. (Num. 11:1–3)
3. I. (1 Kings 18:19–40)
4. N. (Exod. 13:21)
5. O. (Gen. 19:12–29)
6. B. (2 Kings 2:11–12)
7. L. (Judg. 13:20)
8. C. (Isa. 6:6)
9. P. (Gen. 3:24)
10. E. (Judg. 6:21)
11. H. (Dan. 7:9–10)
12. M. (Exod. 9:20–26)
13. A. (Dan. 3:19–20)
14. K. (James 3:6)
15. G. (Acts 2:3–4, 16)
16. D. (Moo 1:2, 3 kick)

Adam's Family
Pages 90-92

1. False (Gen. 1:24–26)
2. True (Gen. 2:7)
3. True (Gen. 2:10, 14)
4. False (Gen. 2:21)
5. False (Gen. 2:16–17)
6. False (Gen. 3:1–5)
7. True (Gen. 3:7)
8. False (Gen. 3:20)
9. True (Gen. 3:16–17)
10. True (Gen. 3:21)
11. False (Gen. 4:25, 5:4)
12. False (Gen. 4:8)
13. True (Gen. 4:14–15)
14. False (Gen. 4:25)
15. True (Gen. 5:5)

16. Unknown. **However, archeologists have discovered an ancient sign in the area, which, when translated, reads: "No girls allowed—even if they haven't been created yet."**

If We Build It … They Will Come! Building Projects of the Bible
Pages 93-94

1. Nimrod **(Gen. 10:8–12)**
2. barns **(Luke 12:18)**
3. his palace **(1 Kings 7:1)**
4. altar **(Josh. 22:10–12)**
5. shelters **(Matt. 17:4)**
6. King David **(2 Sam. 7:1–17)**
7. house **(Prov. 9:1)**
8. the walls of Jerusalem **(Neh. 3:1–6:15)**
9. the temple **(John 2:19–21)**
10. the tower of Babel **(Gen. 11:1–9)**
11. horse
12. Haggai **(Hag. 1:1–8)**
13. Jeroboam **(1 Kings 12:25)**
14. Solomon **(1 Kings 6:1–38)**
15. Sanctuary or tabernacle **(Exod. 25:1–9)**

False Gods Put Idol Hands to Work!
Pages 96-97

1. Baal **(2 Kings 23:5)**
2. a golden calf **(Exod. 32:4–5)**
3. Micah's idols **(Judg. 18:30–31)**
4. Dagon **(1 Sam. 5:1–7)**
5. Molech **(Lev. 18:21; 2 Kings 23:10)**
6. Zeus **(Acts 14:11–13)**
7. Chemosh **(Judg. 11:23–24)**
8. Ashtoreth **(1 Kings 11:5)**
9. Billy Idol
10. Succoth Benoth **(2 Kings 17:30)**
11. Baal **(Judg. 6:25)**
12. Ahaz **(2 Kings 16:3–4)**
13. Anakin (Star Wars: **The Phantom Menace)**

King, Priest, Prophet, or Judge
Pages 98-99

1. prophet (1 Sam. 3:20) judge (1 Sam. 7:15)
2. prophetess (Judg. 4:4) judge (Judg. 2:18; 4:4–5:31)
3. king (1 Kings 16:29)
4. priest (Acts 23:2)
5. prophet (Deut. 18:18)
6. judge (Judg. 2:18; 10:1–2)
7. prophet (Exod. 7:1) priest (Exod. 31:10)
8. king (1 Sam. 11:15)
9. priest (1 Sam. 1:9)
10. prophet (2 Kings 20:1)
11. judge, of course!
12. prophet (Luke 7:26)
13. king (2 Kings 18:1)
14. king (1 Kings 5:1)
15. judge (Judg. 2:18; 6:11–8:32)
16. priest (Ezra 2:2)
17. king, priest (Gen. 14:18)
18. judge (Judg. 2:18; 15:1–20)
19. prophet (1 Kings 18:22)
20. king (2 Kings 24:1)
21. prophet (Jude 14–15)
22. king

Stop Your "Wine-ing"
Pages 100-104

1. D. (Luke 5:37)
2. B. (Num. 6:2–3)
3. B. (Isa. 25:6)
4. A. (Gen. 40:8–13)
5. C. (Prov. 23:32)
6. C. (John 2:1–11)
7. A. (Gen. 9:20–27)
8. D. (1 Tim. 5:23)

9. B. (Esther 1:7–8)
10. A. (Hos. 4:11)
11. C. (Acts 2:13)
12. B, D. (Ps. 75:8)
13. D. (Matt. 26:27–29)
14. A. (Isa. 55:1)
15. B. (Rev. 17:1–2)
16. B. (Luke 10:33–34)
17. C. (Num. 15:4–12)
18. D. (Jer. 13:12)

Farm Out, Man!!!
Pages 105-107

1. True (Exod. 34:21)
2. True (2 Cor. 9:10)
3. False (Amos 7:1)
4. False (James 5:4)
5. False (Ruth 2:3)
6. True (Joel 1:1–20)
7. False (Isa. 5:1–2)
8. False (2 Tim. 2:6)
9. False (The band had broken up during King Saul's reign.)
10. True (Exod. 22:5)
11. True (1 Cor. 9:10)
12. True (Gen. 37:7)
13. False (1 Cor. 3:6)
14. True (John 4:38)
15. True (Prov. 31:16)
16. False (Jer. 50:16)
17. True (Deut. 20:6)
18. False (Hag. 1:11)
19. True (Gen. 2:15)
20. False (Mark 4:31–32)
21. Unknown (Some scholars suggest this may have been edited from the Bible by someone who owned a large block of stock in John Deere.)

Our Town
Pages 109-112

1. Endor (1 Sam. 28:7–8)
2. Bethany (John 11:1–44)
3. Gomorrah (Gen. 19:24–25)
4. Jericho (Josh. 2, 6)
5. Ephesus (Acts 19:1–20)
6. Ai (Josh. 8:1–29)
7. Philippi (Acts 16:12–40)
8. Bethlehem (Gen. 35:19; Ruth 1:19; 1 Sam. 16:1–18)
9. Athens (Acts 17:16–34)
10. Tyre (1 Kings 5:1–12)
11. Joppa (Acts 9:43–10:16)
12. Hebron (Gen. 23:19; 25:8–10)
13. Sidon (Judg. 1:31,10:12; Joel 3:4–6; Mark 7:24–30)
14. Nineveh (2 Kings 19:36; Jon. 1–3)
15. Antioch (Acts 11:20–21)
16. Jerusalem (Gen. 14:18; Ps. 76:2; Matt. 4:5)
17. Cana (John 2:1–11)
18. Gaza (Judg. 16:1–3)
19. Rome (Acts 18:1–2)
20. Shiloh (Judg. 21:16–23)
21. Nazareth (John 1:46)
22. Damascus (Acts 9:1–9)
23. Atlantis

Whose Zoo?
Pages 113-117

1. cobra
2. apes, baboons
3. owls
4. pigs
5. behemoth, leviathan
6. jackals, owls, goats
7. lizard
8. deer
9. camel

10. frogs
11. horses
12. dogs
13. leopard, bear, lion
14. rodents, bats
15. wolf
16. bulls, lion
17. goat
18. foxes
19. colt
20. tarantula (Really?? I thought everyone had one of these.)

JOGGING (YOUR MEMORY!)

WAY TO GO, MO! (PART ONE)

It is a little known fact that the children of Israel often used the nickname "Mo" to refer to their renowned leader, Moses. The truth is (I have this from very reliable sources) that Moses detested the name but considered it the least of his many problems!

The following statements refer to the early days of, and events associated with, Moses. You merely must decide which are true and which are false. That's it, no mo!

_____ 1. The generation of Joseph had all perished prior to the birth of Moses.

_____ 2. The book of Exodus states that God punished the Egyptian midwives for helping to destroy male babies born to the Hebrew women, as commanded by Pharaoh.

_____ 3. Moses' name was given to him by his mother, and means "I put him in the water."

_____ 4. Moses fled to Midian to avoid the possibility of being punished for murder.

_____ 5. Moses and Zipporah's first child was a girl, named Corah.

_____ 6. The "burning bush" encounter was Moses' first visit from God.

_____ 7. God told Moses that his name was "I AM WHO I AM."

_____ 8. As a sign of his ability to help Moses, God made Moses' rod become a serpent, and also made Moses' feet become leprous, then restored them to normal.

_____9. God often called Moses "Mo," just to see if he could get a rise out of him.

_____10. The Lord was planning to kill Moses, but changed his mind after Moses' wife circumcised their son.

_____11. The first time Moses and Aaron met with the leaders of Israel to discuss God's visit, the meeting ended up in disagreement and failure.

_____12. Although Pharaoh was not overly receptive to the first requests of Aaron and Moses, he did somewhat lighten the workload of the Israelites.

_____13. Moses was sixty-eight years old and Aaron was seventy-one when they talked to Pharaoh.

_____14. The magicians of Egypt were able to copy not only the turning of rods into serpents, but also the changing of water into blood.

_____15. Pharaoh agreed to let the Israelites go and sacrifice to God, if Moses would entreat God to end the plague of frogs.

_____16. Even the magicians of Egypt broke out with boils during the sixth plague.

_____17. The seventh plague, hail, destroyed all of the crops of Egypt, which naturally led to famine, the eighth plague.

_____18. God told Moses that the darkness he would send on the land would be so intense, it could actually be felt!

____19. When the children of Israel left Egypt, they took only their own belongings and animals.

____20. Moses carried the bones of Jacob, to honor an oath Jacob had made with the children of Israel.

Wow, looks like you "mowed" right through these! Feel free to "mosey" over to the answers on page 160.

HEY, I'VE GOT SENIORITY! (PART ONE)

Although we're not really certain as to the existence of labor unions during Bible days, some legends have it that the UAW (United Ark Workers) gave Noah fits at the bargaining table. The AFL/CIO (Ax Fellowship of Lebanon/Carpenters of Israel Organization) were also fabled to be tough negotiators when Solomon started his building projects.

The rights of eldest sons (primogeniture) and traditions regarding daughters are also well documented in various Bible stories. Therefore, let's see if you can decide who was "here first" in this list of Bible characters.

Give this some serious effort! Twenty men and women of the earliest part of the Old Testament are included. Arrange them in order of who was born first, second, etc.

Lot	Deborah	Samuel	Enoch
Leah	Samson	Abraham	Cain
Moses	Isaac	Abel	Saul
Joseph	Noah	Ruth	Nimrod
Dinah	Gideon	Joshua	Methuselah

Your list:

1._____

2._____

3._____

4._____

5._____

6._____

7._____

8._____

9._____

10._____

11._____

12._____

13._____

14._____   18._____

15._____   19._____

16._____   20._____

17._____

If you have these arranged perfectly, you may want to consider a career as a florist. (Your fresh-cut answers are displayed on page 160.)

Usually when we read about the plagues God inflicted on ancient Egypt, we don't think too literally about the possible implications. Let's do that now, as I offer you a list of the

TOP TEN CONSEQUENCES OF EGYPTIAN WATER BEING TURNED TO BLOOD

10. Created additional problems for laundry sorting
9. Tended to clot when gargled
8. Allowed Egyptian Red Cross to cancel blood drives
7. Created new kinds of fish: red roughie, red gills, etc.
6. "Bloody Mary" took on a whole new meaning
5. Even innocent people now had blood on their hands
4. Showering created redheads, rednecks, and redeye
3. Added a whole new dimension to coffee
2. Hair washing gave birth to the term "strawberry blonde"
1. You could actually GET blood out of a turnip!

TRICK OR TREE'D?

No, the next quiz has nothing to do with Halloween. Let's try something else:

> *"I think that you will prob'ly see
> A question or two about a tree."*

Okay, I'm going out on a limb here, just leaf it to me. After all, Bible trivia is my branch of literature.

Match the correct tree with the appropriate clue.

(Don't worry, my bark is worse than my bite.)

Here is your list of trees:

pomegranate	terebinth	balsam
oak	cedar	myrtle
palm	adultree	broom
apple	olive	acacia
poplar	fig	infantree
sycamore	cypress	

1. Zacchaeus climbed this tree in order to see Jesus.

    Answer: _____

2. Deborah held court under this kind of tree while judging Israel.

    Answer: _____

3. David's conquest of the Philistines involved specific instructions from God regarding what tree?

    Answer: _____

God's kingdom.

    Answer: _____

5. Solomon apparently made this type of tree very plentiful in his kingdom. (Hint: well-known tree of Lebanon.)

    Answer: _____

6. Gideon presented a sacrifice to the angel of the Lord beneath this species of tree.

    Answer: _____

7. Elijah sat down under one of these trees and prayed that he would die.

    Answer: _____

8. The wood of this tree was used for building the tabernacle.

    Answer: _____

9. King David had a major problem due to this "tree."

    Answer: _____

10. Paul told the Romans that they were originally cut out of this "wild" tree.

    Answer: _____

11. Saul was sitting under a _____ tree when his son Jonathan and Jonathan's armor-bearer slipped out of camp to confront the Philistine garrison.

    Answer: _____

12. When Nehemiah instructed the people to build booths (shelters) in which to reside while listening to the reading of the law, they were to bring branches of olive, palm, and _____ trees.

    Answer: _____

13. In Song of Solomon, the Shulammite woman (bride) is considered to be like this tree, when it is compared to the "trees of the forest."

    Answer: _____

14. God told Isaiah that the cities would be laid waste, except for a few people, who symbolically would represent the stump of a _____ or an oak tree.

     Answer: _____

15. While the King James Bible states that Noah was commanded to build the ark with "gopher wood," later translations identify it as wood from this tree.

     Answer: _____

16. According to Isaiah 44, the Lord said that the descendants of Jacob will spring up like "_____s by the flowing streams."

     Answer: _____

17. According to "Unusual Science Magazine" every mature tree in the world started out as an _____.

     Answer: _____

   Wood you like to see the answers? Well, you only have to ax me once! We stick'd 'em on page 161.

FROM ME . . . TO YOU!

All of the following involve gifts. Match the correct person with the description of what they gave or received.
Here are your people:

Paul	Joseph	Jeremiah
Job	Abigail	Achish, King of Gath
Rebekah	Jesus	Melchizedek
the Philippians	Mordecai	the apostle John
the prodigal son	Red Cross	the daughter of Tyre
Peter	blood bank	Herodias's daughter
David	Caleb	the Queen of Sheba
		wise men from the East

1. His daughter asked for "springs of water" as a gift, and he complied with her wishes.

   Answer: _____

2. He was released by Nebuzaradan, captain of the Babylonian guard, who gave him "provisions and a present" in parting.

   Answer: _____

3. He reminded his younger "apprentice" to "fan into flame the gift of God which is in you through the laying on of my hands."

   Answer: _____

4. She asked for the head of John the Baptist (on a platter) and received it.

   Answer: _____

5. With Pharaoh's approval, he gave his brothers carts, provisions, garments, and more.

Answer: _____

6. He received a tenth of all the spoils from Abraham's victory over Khederlaomer, King of Elam.

   Answer: _____

7. He said to a lame man, "Silver or gold I do not have, but what I do have, I give you." Then he healed the man's infirmity.

   Answer: _____

8. The Lord gave him twice as much as he originally had.

   Answer: _____

9. Paul told these Christians that they were the only ones who sent gifts when he left Macedonia.

   Answer: _____

10. Give the gift of life.

    Answer: _____

11. She gave a gift of much bread, wine, dressed sheep (as opposed to "undressed sheep"), grain, raisins, and figs to David and his men—then became David's wife.

    Answer: _____

12. God told him, "To him who is thirsty I will give to drink without cost from the spring of the water of life."

    Answer: _____

13. He was given a robe, sandals, and a ring.

    Answer: _____

14. She received silver and gold jewelry, as well as clothing, from Abraham's servant.

    Answer: _____

15. He said, "If you, then, though you are evil, know how to give good gifts to your children, how much more will your Father in heaven give good gifts to those that ask him!"

    Answer: _____

16. There had never been such an abundance of spices as when she gave them as a gift to King Solomon.

    Answer: _____

17. He wrote to all the Jews in the provinces nearby, telling them to celebrate the Feast of Purim by giving gifts to each other, and also to the poor.

    Answer: _____

18. They brought gifts of gold, frankincense, and myrrh to the child Jesus.

    Answer: _____

19. He gave David the town of Ziklag.

    Answer: _____

20. If the "daughter" described in Psalm 45 worships her Lord, who will be there with a gift?

    Answer: _____

21. After raiding the Amalekites, he shared the spoils with several tribes in his "stomping grounds."

    Answer: _____

Now turn to page 161 for your gift: the answers!

TOP TEN REASONS GOD CHOSE
MT. SINAI TO ISSUE THE TEN COMMANDMENTS

10. Mt. Everest tough to climb in a robe and sandals
9. "Sunshine Mountain" didn't actually exist
8. Tram up Pike's Peak was temporarily shut down
7. Figured if the bear could make it over, so could Moses
6. Swiss Alps too pricey
5. Could keep an eye on Saddam from there
4. Figured the "mountains of Busch" might complicate things further
3. Was saving Vesuvius for later
2. It started as a molehill; then the Israelites came along
1. Moses was lousy at rappelling

WHEN GOD SPEAKS . . . PEOPLE LISTEN!
(PART ONE)
(Genesis through First Samuel)

Well, at least **sometimes.** And that's not to infer that they necessarily always **obey.** What proceeds is a collection of facts relating to times that God spoke (either directly or through miraculous means) to people of the Bible. Unfortunately, some are true and some are false. Any questions? Good!

_____ 1. The first question God asked Adam after he and Eve had eaten the forbidden fruit was, "Who told you that you were naked?"

_____ 2. Prior to Noah, the last man God had spoken to was Enoch, who "walked with God, then he was no more, because God took him away."

_____ 3. God's initial discourse to Abram (Abraham) involved instructions to remain in the land of Haran until Sarai (Sarah) gave birth to Isaac.

_____ 4. The Lord spoke with Hagar (Sarah's servant) about her unborn son Ishmael, while an angel of the Lord spoke to Sarah about her "old age" pregnancy.

_____ 5. The Lord said to Rachel: "Two nations are in your womb, and two peoples from within you will be separated."

_____ 6. God came to Laban the Aramean (Jacob's father-in-law) in a dream, and told him "not to say anything to Jacob, either good or bad."

_____7. Although Joseph spoke often of God, the Scriptures do not record an instance of God speaking literally to Joseph.

_____8. God's first words to Moses were: "I have indeed seen the misery of my people in Egypt."

_____9. After the Israelites were safely beyond the Red Sea and Egypt, God's next instructions to them involved a promise to keep them free of the diseases brought on Egypt in return for their allegiance to him.

_____10. God's last commands to Moses in the book of Exodus concern the anointing of the priests.

_____11. When God was upset at Moses, he often gave Moses the "silent treatment."

_____12. In the book of Leviticus, God dictates the laws governing worship, diet, sexuality, social order, feasts and more. God always gives these laws to Moses, and Moses alone.

_____13. Moses took the first census reported in the book of Numbers because God told him to.

_____14. In Numbers 12, the Lord spoke to Miriam to tell her how pleased he was with her.

_____15. God's first conversation with Balaam concerned Balaam's previous cruelty to the Israelites.

_____16. Unlike the earlier four books of Moses, the book of Deuteronomy only refers to instances when God talked directly with humans.

____17. After Moses' death, the next person to hear directly from God was Rahab the prostitute.

____18. When the children of Israel asked the Lord who would go up to fight the Canaanites on their behalf (after Joshua's death), the Lord answered, "Judah is to go; I have given the land into their hands."

____19. The Bible says that the first time Samuel heard the Lord speak, "he immediately recognized the voice of his God."

____20. Even though God instructed David to attack the Philistines at Keilah, David asked him a second time if he should go.

____21. God spoke at Samuel's funeral, but didn't allow any pictures to be taken.

And now, **I'm** telling **you** that the solutions are on page 162.

BOOK 'EM DAN-O . . .
THE WHOLE CONGREGATION!

Okay, you'll need an explanation here, so listen carefully. All of the following questions involve issues with various groups of "believers" (a word sometimes used rather loosely), which are also known as "congregations." The "book 'em" part simply means your task is to name the book of the Bible in which the incident takes place. Since I'm not offering multiple choice selections, I will allow you to use an index listing the books of the Bible. But that's it! No cheating. Of course, **I** won't know if you do or not, but **Someone** will. Now really . . . do you want to take that chance?

1. In his book, he cautioned the church of his day to be careful about giving the best seats to the rich who dressed in fine clothes, and dishonoring the poor by making them stand, or sit in a lowly place.

   Book: _____

2. This prophet says: "The prophets prophesy lies, the priests rule by their own authority, and my people love it this way. But what will you do in the end?"

   Book: _____

3. In this book, Paul told this congregation (which did fairly well, actually!) to "work out your salvation with fear and trembling" and "do everything without complaining or arguing."

   Book: _____

4. The people turned to false gods every time the appointed leader died, causing God to become angry and state: "Because this nation has violated the

covenant that I laid down for their forefathers and has not listened to me, I will no longer drive out before them any of the nations Joshua left when he died."

Book: _____

5. In this book, God told Moses that "no foreigner" was to participate in the Passover.

Book: _____

6. This congregation was criticized sharply for mishandling the Lord's Supper: "For as you eat, each of you goes ahead without waiting for anybody else. One remains hungry, another gets drunk."

Book: _____

7. Here, the priests and ministers are charged to "Declare a holy fast; call a sacred assembly. Summon the elders and all who live in the land to the house of the Lord your God, and cry out to the Lord. Alas for that day! For the day of the Lord is near."

Book: _____

8. Here we find a congregation of 144,000 blameless men! (Hard to believe, eh?)

Book: _____

9. Your brother has sinned against you. You try to talk to him but he refuses to listen. You go to him with one or two witnesses; he tells you to take a long walk on a short pier. Finally, you take the matter to the church.

Book: _____

10. "[A]ll the people assembled as one man in the square before the Water Gate [way before Nixon!]. They told

Ezra the scribe to bring out the Book of the Law of Moses."

Book: _____

11. Paul called members of this congregation "foolish" and asked them: "Who has bewitched you?"

Book: _____

12. In this book, an evil woman who despised all the people peered into a looking glass and said, "Mirror, mirror on the wall, who's the fairest of them all?"

Book: _____

13. "The Lord said to Moses, 'Bring Aaron and his sons, their garments, the anointing oil, the bull for the sin offering, the two rams and the basket containing bread made without yeast, and gather the entire assembly at the entrance to the Tent of Meeting.'"

Book: _____

14. God called him to go to the Israelites, "a rebellious nation" that is "obstinate and stubborn" and who "have been in revolt against me to this very day."

Book: _____

15. Jesus "had compassion on them [the multitudes], because they were like sheep without a shepherd."

Book: _____

16. Paul tells the church that if someone has caused them grief, they (rather than severely punish) "ought to forgive and comfort him, so that he will not be overwhelmed by excessive sorrow."

Book: _____

17. Within the Israelite congregation, the people were not to charge interest on "money or food or anything else that may earn interest." However, interest could be charged to a "foreigner."

    Book: _____

18. His book records that "the prophet Hananiah son of Azzur, . . . said to me in the house of the LORD in the presence of the priests and all the people: 'This is what the LORD Almighty, the God of Israel, says: "I will break the yoke of the king of Babylon."'"

    Book: _____

19. Paul encouraged this group of believers, "Live in harmony with one another. Do not be proud, but be willing to associate with people of low position. Do not be conceited."

    Book: _____

20. In this book, the author mentions a man named Diotrephes, who had maliciously put good people out of the church.

    Book: _____

21. The number of Jesus' followers was growing rapidly, and the Twelve (apostles) suggested appointing seven men of good reputation to oversee serving tables, so that the Twelve could give their full attention to prayer and the ministry of the word of God. Now get this: the Bible says that "this proposal pleased the whole group!"

    Book: _____

Congregation, please rise and turn to page 163 for the answers.

ASSAULT & FLATTERY
(A Bible "WhoDunnit!")

As the title implies, these "multiple-guess" questions concern either assaults and attacks or incidents of flattery. You just happen to be the nicest person who's ever purchased this book. Now please don't hurt me!

1. She accused Joseph of sexual assault because he had refused her flattering advances.

   A. Rahab
   B. Jezebel
   C. Tamar, the daughter–in-law of Judah
   D. The wife of Potiphar
   E. Cher (after her split with Sonny)

2. Paul told this group of believers that "we never used flattery, nor did we put on a mask to cover up greed— God is our witness."

   A. The Romans
   B. The Thessalonians
   C. The Ephesians
   D. The Philippians

3. Forty-two of them were assaulted by bears after Elisha cursed them for mocking his baldness!

   A. Soldiers of Joram
   B. Youths from Bethel
   C. Thieves and robbers from Samaria
   D. False prophets of Baal
   E. Rogaine salesmen

4. In Psalm 12, whom did David say had "vanished from among men"? David explained further that "Everyone

lies to his neighbor; their flattering lips speak with deception."

   A. The faithful
   B. "My enemies"
   C. The few
   D. The proud
   E. The Marines

5. His "bow and arrow" assault on King Joram resulted in the arrow piercing his heart and the king's subsequent death.

   A. Nimrod
   B. Hazael king of Syria
   C. Jehu son of Jehoshaphat, the son of Nimshi
   D. Ahab
   E. Robin Hood

6. Paul informed the believers in Rome that those who flatter "to deceive the minds of naive people" do not serve Jesus Christ, but rather serve

   A. The prince of darkness
   B. The shadows of Hades
   C. Wicked leaders in high places
   D. Their own appetites

7. According to Matthew's account of the arrest of Jesus, who took a sword and cut off the ear of the high priest's servant?

   A. Peter
   B. James son of Zebedee
   C. Judas
   D. An unnamed companion
   E. The servant did it himself, after hearing Mark Antony say, "Friends, Romans, countrymen, lend me your ears"

8. A woman pretending to be a mourner flattered this king, telling him that his ability to discern good and evil "is like an angel of God."

    A. David
    B. Solomon
    C. Ahab
    D. Zechariah

9. He was assaulted and killed by his own sons "while he was worshiping in the temple of his god Nisroch."

    A. Nebuchadnezzar
    B. Sennacherib
    C. Hezekiah
    D. Cyrus

10. In Mark 12, men from two different groups were sent to Jesus to "catch him in his words." Before asking him their trick question, they attempted to flatter him. What two groups did they represent?

    A. Pharisees and Herodians
    B. Scribes and Sadducees
    C. Helenists and tax collectors
    D. Lawyers and teachers
    E. The harpists union and the idol manufacturers

11. Five kings hid in a cave to avoid the fury of Joshua's army. Joshua sealed off the cave for a while, then later brought them out and "struck and killed the kings." Which of the following is NOT one of those kings?

    A. The king of Jerusalem
    B. The king of Hebron
    C. The king of Jericho
    D. The king of Jarmuth
    E. The king of Lachish
    F. The king of Eglon

12. Solomon says that "the wayward wife with her seductive words, who has left the partner of her youth," ignores what?

   A. The virtue of her mother
   B. The commandments of her father
   C. That Sheol awaits the wicked
   D. The covenant she made before God
   E. That you may be on the vice squad

13. Acts 12 says that Herod decided to "arrest some who belonged to the church." Who was the first to be struck down by him?

   A. Stephen
   B. Peter
   C. James, the brother of John
   D. John, the brother of James
   E. Dr. Joyce Brothers

14. "If I have now found favor in your eyes, accept this gift from me. For to see your face is like seeing the face of God, now that you have received me favorably." Who is speaking this apparently earnest bit of flattery?

   A. Lot is speaking to Abraham
   B. Jacob is speaking to Esau
   C. Ruth is speaking to Boaz
   D. Esther is speaking to King Xerxes
   E. Martha Stewart is speaking to the grand jury

15. He watched the king of Babylon's men murder his sons; then they put out his eyes and carried him off to Babylon.

   A. Bartimaeus
   B. King Zedekiah
   C. Haman
   D. Gedaliah, the governor

16. Daniel prophesies: "With flattery he will corrupt those who have violated the covenant, but the people who know their God will firmly resist him." To whom does the **he** refer?

A. An unnamed king
B. King Cyrus of Persia
C. Darius the Mede
D. Nebuchadnezzar

Now it's time to find out if flattery will get you anywhere. (And I don't recommend assault if it doesn't!) Either way, the answers are on page 163.

INHALE, EXILE, INHALE, EXILE

The following locations are all associated with exile because the individuals either:

A. were sent there against their will, or
B. went there due to fear of what might happen to them if they stayed.

Match the following people with the exilic circumstances with which they are associated. (Miss more than half and **you** will be sent away!)

David	the apostle John	Adam & Eve
Jeremiah	Cain	Daniel
Jephthah	Manasseh	Jacob
Absalom	Hagar & Ishmael	Moses
Ezekiel	Jeroboam	Jehoiachin

1. While in captivity, he was selected as part of an elite group to be taught "the language and literature of the Babylonians."

    Answer: _____

2. When exiled by the Lord, he dwelt in the land of Nod. (If you know the answer, shake your head up and down.)

    Answer: _____

3. He was carted off to Babylon in shackles. Eventually, he made it back to Jerusalem.

    Answer: _____

4. He had several profound visions while exiled on an island called Patmos.

    Answer: _____

5. While hiding from the king of Israel, he spent some time in the cave of Adullam.

    Answer: _____

6. These TWO individuals were banished by Abraham and wandered in the wilderness of Beersheba.

    Answer: _____

7. He was driven out of the house by his half-brothers and went to the land of Tob.

    Answer: _____

8. After ordering the murder of Amnon, he fled into exile for several years.

    Answer: _____

9. He was carried off to Egypt with all "the remnant of Judah who had come back to live in the land of Judah."

    Answer: _____

10. This man, who would later become king of Israel, fled to Egypt to avoid the potential wrath of Solomon.

    Answer: _____

11. They were exiled from a relatively small area to a very large one, then essentially set free.

    Answer: _____

12. He ran away to Midian to escape capital punishment for murder.

    Answer: _____

13. While he was "among the exiles by the Kebar River, the heavens were opened and [he] saw visions of God."

    Answer: _____

14. He was in captivity thirty-seven years, before King Evil-Merodach released him from prison.

    Answer: _____

15. His father sent him away to a place called Paddan Aram.

    Answer: _____

Waiting to exile? Oops, I mean **exhale.** It's okay—relax and turn to page 164 to see how they're supposed to match.

"Solomon here, to welcome you to the end of chapter four. And this time, I've decided not to sing. Instead, I'm going to pass on some little-known family information about my father, David. According to what Dad told me about his ordeal with that infamous giant, here are the

TOP TEN THINGS DAVID DID BEFORE FACING GOLIATH

10. Put thirty-shot clip in sling
9. Called his attorney, Mr. Cohen, with instructions regarding his will
8. Changed into his worst pair of underwear
7. Returned his cell phone
6. Had family portraits taken
5. Gave away his baseball card collection
4. Put a hold on his mail
3. Went skydiving
2. Hid a knife in his boot
1. Ran up all of his credit cards

"And now, here's one of my all-time favorite females to close the chapter. She's the only woman I know who was named by her husband! Let's give it up for Eve!"
(Applause, please!)

"Thanks, Solomon. Actually, my husband, Adam, wanted to have lots of wives just like you. His only problem was, he didn't have enough ribs!
"And many of you may not realize that Adam and I still got into a lot of trouble AFTER we were evicted from Eden. You see, we were always raising Cain! (rim shot)

"Of course, the great thing about being the first couple was that we never had any trouble with our in-laws!

"Wow, you're a great crowd! I'll see you in chapter five. In the meantime, can I tempt you with some apple pie?"

JOGGING (YOUR MEMORY!)
ANSWERS

Way to Go, Mo!
Pages 129-131

_____ 1. True (Exod. 1:6)
_____ 2. False (Exod. 1:20–21)
_____ 3. False (Exod. 2:10)
_____ 4. True (Exod. 2:12–15)
_____ 5. False (Exod. 2:22)
_____ 6. True (Exod. 3:2)
_____ 7. True (Exod. 3:13–14)
_____ 8. False (Exod. 4:1–9)
_____ 9. True (Dead Sea Videotapes)
_____ 10. True (Exod. 4:24–26)
_____ 11. False (Exod. 4:29–31)
_____ 12. False (Exod. 5:1–23)
_____ 13. False (Exod. 7:7)
_____ 14. True (Exod. 7:10–11, 20–22)
_____ 15. True (Exod. 8:8)
_____ 16. True (Exod. 9:11)
_____ 17. False (Exod. 9:32)
_____ 18. True (Exod. 10:21)
_____ 19. False (Exod. 12:35–36)
_____ 20. False (Exod. 13:19)

Hey, I've Got Seniority!
Pages 132-133

1. Cain (Gen. 4:1).
2. Abel (Gen. 4:1)
3. Enoch (Gen. 4:17; 5:18–24)
   (Note: There were actually two Enochs; one was the first
   son of Cain, and the other the father of Methuselah. It is
   this latter Enoch whom the Bible seems to indicate was
   taken directly by God without experiencing physical death.
   Both of these Enochs fit into this time line accurately, and
   man, am I glad!)
4. Methuselah (Gen. 5:21)
5. Noah (Gen. 5:28–29)
6. Nimrod (Gen. 10:8)
7. Abraham (Gen. 11:26)

8. Lot (Gen. 11:27)
9. Isaac (Gen. 21:2–3)
10. Leah (Gen. 29:16)
11. Dinah (Gen. 30:21; 34:1)
12. Joseph (Gen. 30:22–24)
13. Moses (Exod. 2:1–10)
14. Joshua (Exod. 24:13; Josh. 1:1–20)
15. Deborah (Judg. 4:4)
16. Gideon (Judg. 6:11)
17. Samson (Judg. 13:24)
18. Ruth (Ruth 1:4)
19. Samuel (1 Sam. 1:20)
20. Saul (1 Sam. 9:2; 12:1)

Trick or Tree'd?
Pages 135-137

1. sycamore (Luke 19:4)
2. palm (Judg. 4:4–5)
3. balsam (2 Sam. 5:23–25)
4. fig (Matt. 24:32)
5. cedar (1 Kings 10:27)
6. oak (Judg. 6:19)
7. broom (1 Kings 19:4)
8. acacia (Exod. 36:20)
9. adultree (2 Sam. 11)
10. olive (Rom. 11:24)
11. pomegranate (1 Sam. 14:2)
12. myrtle (Neh. 8:15)
13. apple (Song of Sol. 2:3)
14. terebinth (Isa. 6:13)
15. cypress (Gen. 6:14)
16. poplar (Isa. 44:4)
17. infantree (sorry!)

From Me . . . To You!
Pages 138-140

1. Caleb (Judg. 1:13–15)
2. Jeremiah (Jer. 40:5)

3. Paul (2 Tim. 1:6)
4. Herodias's daughter (Mark 6:22–28)
5. Joseph (Gen. 45:21)
6. Melchizedek (Gen. 14:17–20)
7. Peter (Acts 3:6–8)
8. Job (Job 42:10)
9. the Philippians (Phil. 4:15)
10. Red Cross blood bank (I'm positive)
11. Abigail (1 Sam. 25:18,27)
12. the apostle John (Rev. 21:6)
13. the prodigal son (Luke 15:22)
14. Rebekah (Gen. 24:53)
15. Jesus (Matt. 7:11)
16. The Queen of Sheba (1 Kings 10:10)
17. Mordecai (Esther 9:20–22)
18. Wise men from the east (Matt. 2:1–11)
19. Achish, King of Gath (1 Sam. 27:5–6)
20. the daughter of Tyre (Ps. 45:11–12)
21. David (1 Sam. 30:18–31)

When God Speaks … People Listen! (Part One)
(Genesis through first Samuel)
Pages142-144

1. False (Gen. 3:9–11)
2. True (Gen. 5:24)
3. False (Gen. 12:1–3)
4. False (Gen. 16:7–12; 18:1–15)
5. False (Gen. 25:21–23)
6. True (Gen. 31:24)
7. True (Gen. 37–50)
8. False (Exod. 3:4–7)
9. True (Exod. 15:26)
10. True (Exod. 40:15)
11. Other than thunder and lightning, of course
12. False (Lev. 13:1; 14:33; 15:1)
13. True (Num. 1:1–2)
14. False (Num. 12:1–16)
15. False (Num. 22:9–12)

16. True (Deut. 1:1–3)
17. False (Josh. 1:1–2)
18. True (Judg. 1:1–2)
19. False (1 Sam. 3:1–10)
20. True (1 Sam. 23:1–4)
21. Per legend only!

Book 'em Dan-O
Pages 145-148

1. James (2:1–6)
2. Jeremiah (5:31)
3. Philippians (2:12–14)
4. Judges (2:18–21)
5. Exodus (12:43)
6. 1 Corinthians (11:21)
7. Joel (1:14–15)
8. Revelation (14:1–5)
9. Matthew (18:15–17)
10. Nehemiah (8:1)
11. Galatians (3:1)
12. Snow White
    (Note: If you find this book in your Bible, you have a very
    rare Bible. Only five are known to exist.)
13. Leviticus (8:1–3)
14. Ezekiel (2:3–6)
15. Mark (6:34)
16. 2 Corinthians (2:5–7)
17. Deuteronomy (23:19–20)
18. Jeremiah (28:1–2)
19. Romans (12:16)
20. 3 John (9–10)
21. Acts (6:1–5)

Assault & Flattery
Pages 149-153

1. D. (Gen. 39:6–20)
2. B. (1 Thess. 2:5)
3. B. (2 Kings 2:23–24)

4. A. (Ps. 12:1–2)
5. C. (2 Kings 9:14–24)
6. D. (Rom. 16:18)
7. D. (Matt. 26:51)
8. A. (2 Sam. 14:17)
9. B. (Isa. 37:37–38)
10. A. (Mark 12:13–17)
11. C. (Josh. 10:22–26)
12. D. (Prov. 2:16–17)
13. C. (Acts 12:1–2)
14. B. (Gen. 33:10)
15. B. (2 Kings 25:7)
16. A. (Dan. 11:32)

Inhale, Exile
Pages 154-156

1. Daniel (Dan. 1:1–6)
2. Cain (Gen. 4:3–16)
3. Manasseh (2 Chron. 33:11–13)
4. John (Rev. 1:9)
5. David (1 Sam. 22:1)
6. Hagar & Ishmael (Gen. 21:14)
7. Jephthah (Judg. 11:3)
8. Absalom (2 Sam. 13:37–38)
9. Jeremiah (Jer. 43:5–7)
10. Jeroboam (1 Kings 11:40)
11. Adam & Eve (Gen. 3:24)
12. Moses (Exod. 2:15)
13. Ezekiel (Ezek. 1:1–2)
14. Jehoiachin (2 Kings 25:27–30)
15. Jacob (Gen. 28:1–5)

5

HITTING YOUR STRIDE

(I don't recommend this if your stride is bigger than you are.)

GETTING INTO THE ACT

The questions that follow involve the great (or maybe not-so-great) actors of the Bible: people who pretended to be someone other than who or what they were. As is my habit, I've gotten some of these facts wrong **intentionally.** It's **true** or **false** time again! Remember: In order to be true, the entire statement must be accurate.

___1.   Amnon, a son of David, pretended to be sick so that he could force his half-sister, Tamar, to go to bed with him.

___2.   Rachel posed as her sister Leah, and fooled Jacob on their wedding night. (It was very dark.)

___3.   A prophet who disguised himself with a bandage over his eyes told someone to hit him so he could appear wounded.

___4.   Some of the Pharisees' disciples came with the Herodians to trick Jesus with a question about paying taxes, pretending to be sincere inquirers.

___5.   To make certain he wouldn't be found out when he went to visit the medium, Saul disguised himself and went alone to Endor.

___6.   Since Abram was concerned that his wife Sarai's beauty could cost him his life in Egypt, she agreed to pretend to be his cousin.

___7.   Before the demon-possessed swine ran into the sea, they actually had been part of the "Palestinian Porkers" Synchronized Swimming Team.

___8. Because David feared the king of Gath, he pretended to be insane, scratching on the gate doors and letting saliva drip down his beard.

___9. When Herod heard about Jesus, he was certain that Jesus was the prophet Elijah risen from the grave.

__10. When Absalom called the woman from Tekoa to visit his father, he instructed her to wear mourning apparel and act the part of a grieving mother.

__11. While it's true that Jacob managed to steal his brother Esau's birthright by falsely posing as his older brother, it's also true that Rebekah, his mother, planned the whole scheme.

__12. The Gibeonites, one of the nations that Joshua was trying to conquer, managed to trick him into a peace treaty by pretending to be from a far country.

__13. When King Jeroboam's wife was very ill, he instructed his son to disguise himself and go seek Ahijah the prophet.

__14. Herod tried to convince the shepherds to tell him the location of Jesus' birth, under the pretense that he, too, wanted to worship the Child.

__15. King Josiah was mortally wounded after disguising himself and going to battle against the king of Egypt.

__16. King Ahab died after riding in a chariot posing as an armored soldier.

Now, to check the accuracy of your work, which you pretended to take so seriously, advance to page 198.

WE ARE WOMEN—HEAR US ROAR

I love women. In fact, I love women so much that I married one. (Solomon **really** loved women.) Anyway, it's time to think about the ladies of the Bible and appreciate their contributions. Match the women from the list that follows with the descriptions that correctly correspond to their name. You go, girl!

Miriam	Cozbi	Elizabeth	Lois
Mary Magdalene	Joanna	Gomer	Abigail
Candace	Anna	Dinah	Vashti
Phoebe	Mary	Hannah	Rizpah
Naomi	Zeresh	Keturah	Jezebel
Merab	Damaris	Michal	Jochebed

1. When her husband, who also happened to be the king of Persia, summoned her to his party, she was a no-show!

    Answer: _____

2. This Athenian woman was one of Paul's converts.

    Answer: _____

3. She wasn't afraid to rebel, and once she was punished with leprosy and confined outside the Israelite camp for a week.

    Answer: _____

4. Saul's older daughter was promised to David, but was given to Adriel of Meholah instead.

    Answer: _____

5. She was the wife of Cuza, Herod's household manager, and had been healed by Jesus.

    Answer: _____

6. King David had both a sister and a wife with this name.

    Answer: _____

7. At about eighty-four years of age, this widow and prophetess had an opportunity to see the Christ Child.

    Answer: _____

8. This Midianite woman was killed, along with her Israelite "gentleman-friend," by the javelin of Aaron's grandson, Phinehas.

    Answer: _____

9. Paul called her "our sister," "a servant in the church of Cenchrea."

    Answer: _____

10. When God instructed Hosea to marry an adulterous woman, he obeyed and married this one. (He picked her up at "A Mart"—she was a "red-light" special.)

    Answer: _____

11. Some time after the death of Sarah, Abraham took a wife who bore him six children. What was her name?

    Answer: _____

12. Because she had previously been unable to bear children, she was elated at the thought of being pregnant. Then she gave birth to John the Baptist.

    Answer: _____

13. This woman, a concubine of Saul, protected the corpses of Saul's descendants who had been hanged by the Gibeonites.

    Answer: _____

14. The price David paid to become King Saul's son-in-law was two hundred Philistine foreskins. Then he was given _____, Saul's daughter. (Fortunately for the Philistine men involved, David had mercy on them, and killed them before the surgery.)

    Answer: _____

15. Because "the Almighty has made my life very bitter," she told the people not to call her by her former name, but instead to call her Mara.

    Answer: _____

16. Philip's conversation about Jesus Christ with the Ethiopian treasurer led to his conversion and baptism. What was the name of the Ethiopian queen he served?

    Answer: _____

17. Unfortunately, some women end up being married to villains. So is the case with her; her husband was Haman.

    Answer: _____

18. This daughter of Jacob was "violated" by a Hivite man, leading to a bevy of problems.

    Answer: _____

19. She was "deeply troubled," but the priest accused her of being drunk!

    Answer: _____

20. She was the mother of Moses.

    Answer: _____

21. At the wedding of Cana, she told Jesus that there was no wine.

    Answer: _____

22. She died after being tossed out an upstairs window by "two or three eunuchs."

    Answer: _____

23. Matthew's account names her first among those visiting Jesus Christ's tomb after his burial.

    Answer: _____

24. When Paul talked of Timothy's faith, he mentioned that it had been passed down to him from his grandmother. What was her name?

    Answer: _____

Let's see how well you fared on our little "Name that Dame Game." You'll find the femmes on page 198.

IT'S A LIVING (PART TWO)

Only this time, we'll make it (heh heh) multiple choice. Good luck!

1. Othni, Rephael, and Obed served as

    A. Stable attendants to Solomon
    B. Sanctuary gatekeepers
    C. Sculptors/artisans
    D. Teachers of the law

2. According to Romans 16, Erastus was a

    A. City director of public works
    B. Counselor to Pilate
    C. Philosopher
    D. Shepherd
    E. Bouncer at the Coliseum

3. The Bible says that God was with the lad Ishmael, and he became

    A. A great hunter
    B. A warrior
    C. A possessor of much land
    D. An archer
    E. An actuary

4. Lydia, a lady mentioned in the book of Acts, made a living by

    A. Gleaning grain from the wheat fields
    B. Selling purple cloth
    C. Weaving baskets
    D. Making tents
    E. Renting videos

5. Nehemiah worked for the king of Persia. What specifically did he do?

    A. Laundered and cared for the king's wardrobe
    B. Advised the king regarding matters of war
    C. Interpreted the king's dreams
    D. Cupbearer (tasted the king's wine to make sure it wasn't poisoned)

6. Along with the distinction of being the first guy to whack his brother, Cain was also

    A. A man who worked the soil
    B. A digger of wells (water, not Orson)
    C. A hunter of great renown
    D. A keeper of goats
    E. A maker of potato chips

7. According to Paul's letter to Philemon, Onesimus was a

    A. Merchant
    B. Former soldier
    C. Slave
    D. Eunuch (and part of a royal choral group)
    E. Talent scout

8. Joab's occupation involved

    A. Sounding the trumpet upon the king's arrival
    B. Tending the wounded after a battle
    C. Commanding the armies of King David
    D. Driving out the mediums and seers from Israel

9. Although Jesus is known for teaching and healing, he had worked as a

    A. Tentmaker
    B. Carpenter
    C. Copier of the Law
    D. Stonemason
    E. Welder

10. First Kings 21 tells the story of a man named Naboth, who spent his time

   A. Making curtains for Solomon's temple
   B. Tending a vineyard
   C. Crafting drinking vessels of silver
   D. Building ships for Solomon's fleet

11. One of Jesus' twelve disciples, Matthew, worked as a

   A. Jail attendant
   B. Fisherman
   C. Physician
   D. Tax collector
   E. Drummer for Pink Floyd

12. What was Hagar's field of endeavor?

   A. A maidservant
   B. A midwife
   C. A professional mourner
   D. A keeper of goats
   E. She made blue jeans for Levi

13. His name was Felix. He was not a cat. Instead, he was

   A. A Pharisee who debated with Jesus
   B. A temple musician
   C. A Greek orator
   D. A Roman governor
   E. A military figure who had been healed by Peter

14. According to 1 Chronicles, one of the contemporaries of King David, Asaph, was assigned to be a

   A. Lawgiver (reader of the Law)
   B. Server of food at the temple construction site
   C. Overseer of the temple foundation
   D. Cymbal player

15. Tubal-Cain, who is mentioned early in the book of Genesis, had this as his occupation:

    A. Craftsman in bronze and iron
    B. Maker of long bows and arrows of almond wood
    C. Preparer of animal skins (tanner)
    D. Tender of the Garden of Eden after the expulsion of Adam and Eve
    E. The man who put the "ram" in the "ramma damma ding dong"

16. Caiaphas served as

    A. Secretary to Nero
    B. A high priest
    C. A centurion (leader of 100 men)
    D. A watchman at the temple

17. When the angel of the Lord first called Gideon into service, he was

    A. Threshing wheat
    B. Caring for sheep
    C. Slaughtering a ram
    D. Gathering grapes for wine
    E. Running a small travel agency

18. According to Joshua 13:22, Balaam was considered to be a

    A. Prophet of evil
    B. Builder of idols
    C. False teacher
    D. Practicer of divination

19. The book of Acts mentions a man named Demetrius, who made figurines of the goddess Artemis. What material marked his trade?

    A. Ivory
    B. Copper

C. Brass

D. Silver

E. Silly Putty

20. Abner was a cousin to Saul, and also was

A. Saul's bodyguard

B. Saul's armor bearer

C. The army commander

D. A chariot builder

21. Jezebel was

A. A judge of Israel

B. A prostitute

C. The queen of Israel

D. The queen of Judah

22. The first chapter of Esther tells us that a man named Mehuman served what function?

A. A member of a group of eunuchs who served the king

B. Part of a group of musicians who entertained at the king's festivals

C. The king's royal wine server

D. The king's baker

E. The king's Internet advisor

So, before the headhunters start offering all of our biblical wonders better jobs, let's find out what they really do. (Actually, **headhunters** probably had a much more **literal** implication in Bible days!) To make your task as "answer-checker" as easy as possible, turn to page 199.

How about a Top Ten time out? Let's go back to the Garden of Eden to discover the

TOP TEN WAYS ADAM AND EVE REALIZED THEY WERE NAKED

10. Ostriches buried their heads in the sand every time they walked by
9. Obvious tan lines
8. J.C. Penney catalog running specials on fig leaves
7. Arrested repeatedly for indecent exposure
6. Noticed a sign reading: Eden Park—Clothing Optional
5. Eve got a call from Cher asking for wardrobe advice
4. Began to spot people in the underbrush with binoculars
3. Climbing trees was getting progressively painful
2. The only tailor in the garden held a sign reading: "Will sew for food"
1. Finished first on Mr. Blackwell's "least dressed list"

MY TWO SONS

You won't find anybody resembling Robbie, Chip, or Ernie here; and don't expect Fred MacMurray either.

Just a guy with **two** sons, one of them well known as the prodigal son.

This is the famous parable told by Jesus in Luke 15. All you have to do is put "yes" beside each statement that is a part of the story, and "no" next to each one that isn't. Now, here's your inheritance from Uncle Charlie. Don't blow it!

_____ 1. When the younger son asked for his portion of goods, the father divided his livelihood to both sons.

_____ 2. Jesus said the prodigal son wasted his allotment over a period of "a few months."

_____ 3. After the young man had spent all his money, he became very ill.

_____ 4. Fortunately for the prodigal son, he discovered that he could draw unemployment for at least three months.

_____ 5. His first job involved feeding pigs.

_____ 6. When the prodigal son first considered returning home, he pondered asking his father to take him on as a hired hand.

_____ 7. Since the father had no idea where his son was, the father had his missing son's picture put on all of the milk cartons in Israel.

_____ 8. When the son first arrived home, his father was not there.

____9. The father commanded his servants to bring the prodigal son the best robe, a ring, and sandals.

___10. The father ordered a lamb to be slaughtered and eaten in celebration of his reunion with his son.

___11. The older brother learned what was taking place from one of the servants.

___12. The father was angry at the older brother for not helping celebrate his brother's return.

___13. The older brother accused the father of never giving him a goat so that he could party with his friends.

___14. The father responded by saying, "Son, you're always getting my goat!"

___15. The older son said his brother had wasted the father's livelihood with prostitutes.

___16. The father told his older son that his younger brother had been dead, but was now alive.

___17. When Jesus finished this parable, he explained to his disciples that the prodigal son represented the Jews, who would later reject him, and the older brother signified the Gentiles, who were jealous of the Jews as God's chosen people.

___18. A similar version of this parable also appears in Matthew's Gospel.

For one bonus point, name the dog from "My Three Sons."

And while I'm humming the theme song, you can check the answers on page 199.

MAY I HAVE THIS DANCE?

Now, don't think you're just going to just waltz right in here and get all of these correct. I fully intend to throw in a twist or two to try and keep you off balance until we've both had our filly. Er, I mean **fill.** Good luck . . . now, break a leg!

1. He was chastised by his wife, Michal, for dancing in public like a commoner.

   Answer: _____

2. Her seductive dance before Herod cost John the Baptist his head.

   Answer: _____

3. In Psalm 30, David said, "You turned my _____ into dancing."

   Answer: _____

4. His anger burned when he saw the people in the camp dancing around an idol.

   Answer: _____

5. As they danced, they sang, "Saul has slain his thousands, and David his tens of thousands."

   Answer: _____

6. As he headed in from the field, he heard music and dancing, and was uncertain as to its purpose.

   Answer: _____

7. Jesus compared the generation during his earthly ministry to _____ sitting in the marketplaces and calling to their companions saying, "We played the flute for you, and you did not dance. . . ."

    Answer: _____

8. This judge of Israel returned to his house, where his only child came to meet him, "dancing to the sound of tambourines!"

    Answer: _____

9. In Ecclesiastes, the Teacher says there is a "time to _____ and a time to dance."

    Answer: _____

10. The young men of this tribe waited for the girls of Shiloh to come out to join in the dancing at an annual festival, then kidnapped them and took them as wives.

    Answer: _____

11. She led the women of Israel in a dance to celebrate the crossing of the Red Sea.

    Answer: _____

12. He told his friends that the wicked prosper, that their children dance, and "sing to the music of tambourine and harp."

    Answer: _____

13. These two consecutive psalms both encourage the reader to praise the Lord with dance. Which two?

    Answer: _____

14. "I will build you up again and you will be built, O Virgin Israel. Again you will take up your tambourines and go out to dance with the joyful." What prophet claimed that the Lord had spoken these words to him?

   Answer: _____

Feel free to boogie toward page 200, where you'll find answers for dancers.

HEY, GOOD LOOKIN'

All of these people were mentioned by biblical writers as possessing notable physical attractiveness. This tended to create problems for them. (Glad I don't have to deal with stuff like that!)

Here's your list:

Tamar	Joseph	Bathsheba
Absalom	Sarai	Vashti
Job	the Shulammite woman	David
Moses	Mohammed Ali	Abigail
Samson	Abishag	Rebekah
Rachel	Esther	

1. When her husband wanted to show off her beauty to his drinking buddies, she refused to show up for the party.

    Answer: _____

2. No one in Israel received more praise for his handsome appearance.

    Answer: _____

3. His mother saw that he was "no ordinary child."

    Answer: _____

4. She referred to herself as "dark . . . yet lovely."

    Answer: _____

5. Even though he committed no crime, his good looks ultimately landed him in prison.

    Answer: _____

6. This "very beautiful" virgin lay beside the aged King David's side to keep him warm.

   Answer: _____

7. Her half-brother became so obsessed with her beauty that he forced her to have sex with him.

   Answer: _____

8. She was "lovely in form, and beautiful."

   Answer: _____

9. His father-in-law, after giving away his wife to another man, tried to appease him by saying, "Isn't her younger sister more attractive? Take her instead."

   Answer: _____

10. She was spotted from a distance while bathing, and was "very beautiful."

    Answer: _____

11. He said, "My face is so pretty, you don't see a scar, which proves I'm the king of the ring by far."

    Answer: _____

12. She was an orphan, "was lovely in form and features," and her Hebrew name was Hadassah.

    Answer: _____

13. "The girl was very beautiful, a virgin; no man had ever lain with her." She was also a relative of Abraham.

    Answer: _____

14. His daughters were said to be the most beautiful "in all the land, . . . and [he] granted them an inheritance along with their brothers."

    Answer: _____

15. Her husband was "surly and mean in his dealings," but "she was an intelligent and beautiful woman."

    Answer: _____

16. In his youth, he was described as "ruddy, with a fine appearance and handsome features."

    Answer: _____

17. Her husband told her that her beauty could easily put his life in jeopardy.

    Answer: _____

Most attractive solutions appear on page 201.

TOP TEN ISSUES ADAM FACED
WHEN NAMING THE ANIMALS

10. Ants wanted to be called bears
 9. Cats referred to themselves as "God"
 8. Rabbits didn't care about names
 7. Snakes were still ticked about the crawling deal
 6. Raccoons all asked to be "the Lone Ranger"
 5. Foxes suggested elephants be called "peanut suckers"
 4. Adam knew that Eve would want something to be called "Barbie"
 3. Mules had already named themselves and had no interest in compromising
 2. Parrots kept repeating his worst ideas
 1. Every time he said "hyena" all the animals laughed

SECOND WIVES CLUB

Okay, maybe there weren't as many divorces in Bible times as there are today, but lots of men had "second" wives. This was sometimes due to a death of the first, or simply because a guy happened to be a "collector."

Because I'm in a good mood, I'll make it multiple choice!

1. David's second wife was:

   A. Michal (Saul's daughter)
   B. Ahinoam of Jezreel
   C. Abigail
   D. Bathsheba
   E. David had only one wife, Bathsheba

2. After the death of Sarah, Abraham married a woman named

   A. Shemaiah
   B. Keturah
   C. Sheba
   D. Milcah
   E. Mary Todd

3. Lamech was a great, great, great grandson of Cain. His second wife was

   A. Shamish
   B. Zillah
   C. Adah
   D. Dinah
   E. Jennifer

4. Jacob's second wife actually was supposed to be his first. Who was she?

   A. Bilhah
   B. Zilpah

C. Leah

D. Rachel

5. The second wife of Moses apparently was

   A. An unnamed Cushite woman
   B. A woman named Zipporah
   C. Miriam
   D. His niece
   E. Fairly passive

6. According to Paul's instruction in Romans 7, which of the following occurrences legally freed a married woman to wed another man?

   A. Sexual infidelity on the part of her husband
   B. Her husband's petition for a divorce
   C. Her husband's taking of a second wife
   D. The death of her husband

7. Esau's second wife was

   A. Oholibamah
   B. Basemath
   C. Adah
   D. Korah

   (Apparently Ecame, Esau, Econquered. Do you suppose E got Email?)

8. Boaz was actually the second husband of Ruth. (Yes, I know this is supposed to be Second Wives Club, but cut me a little slack, okay?) Who was Ruth's first husband?

   A. Elimelech
   B. Kilion
   C. Mahlon
   D. Obed

9. Paul told Timothy that he desired the younger widows to remarry and (two answers):

   A. Pray daily
   B. Serve their husbands
   C. Have children
   D. Manage their homes
   E. Housebreak the dog

10. Samson's second wife was

   A. A prostitute from Gaza
   B. Delilah
   C. An unnamed Philistine woman of Timnah
   D. Ramath Lehi
   E. Samson had only one wife

11. Samuel's father, Elkanah, had two wives. One of them was Samuel's mother. The other was

   A. Damaris
   B. Peninnah
   C. Hannah
   D. Gomer

12. David's son Absalom fathered at least four children. They were born to

   A. His first wife
   B. His second wife
   C. Two of his concubines
   D. The Bible doesn't say

13. It is difficult to ascertain who Solomon's second wife was because, after the mention of Pharaoh's daughter as his first wife, the next mention of wives indicates he had accumulated

   A. 150 wives and 30 concubines
   B. 360 wives and 100 concubines

C. 700 wives and 300 concubines

D. 1,200 wives and queens, and 450 concubines

E. Five queens, four wives, three princesses, two concubines, and a partridge in a pear tree

14. This king's second wife, along with his first wife (and probably lots more), were carried off to Babylon by Nebuchadnezzar's army.

A. Josiah

B. Jehoiachin

C. Zedekiah

D. Manasseh

15. Solomon's son Rehoboam reigned after the death of King Solomon. The Bible says that Rehoboam loved his second wife "more than any of his other wives and concubines." Name her.

A. Maachah, a descendant of Absalom

B. Mahalath, granddaughter of David

C. Ziza, an Ethiopian princess

D. Ophir, the daughter of Hiram, king of Lebanon

E. Lulu, daughter of a redneck Moabite named Billy-Bob

16. When this king ditched his first wife for insubordination, he held a "Who Wants to Marry a Multi-Millionaire Persian King?" contest to find a second wife.

A. Mordecai

B. Xerxes

C. Haman

D. Hegai

E. Abagtha

17. This prophet's second wife was the same as his first!

A. Joel

B. Ezekiel

C. Amos

D. Hosea

18. The apostle Paul told Timothy that men seeking either of these two offices should only have one wife (two answers).

A. Pastor
B. Communion server
C. Deacon
D. Psalmist
E. Overseer or elder
F. Chairman of Finance Committee

Check your answers on page 201. Sorry, unlike marriage, no second chances here!

IT'S ALL RELATIVE

Lots of the people in the Bible were related, some too closely for comfort! (It's like the old joke: you might be a redneck if . . . you've been married three times and still have the same in-laws!) Anyway, to make it just a little easier, we'll try this with a true/false format. Good luck!

___ 1. Ruth was David's grandmother.

___ 2. King Melchizedek had no known parents.

___ 3. Lazarus, whom Jesus raised from the dead, was a brother to Mary and Martha.

___ 4. Methuselah, the man who has the highest recorded age (969) of any man in the Bible, had a son named Enoch, who lived 365 years and then was taken away by God.

___ 5. When Nebuchadnezzar conquered Judah in 597 B.C., Jehoiachin of Judah was overthrown and a new king named Zedekiah was installed in his place. Zedekiah was actually Jehoiachin's uncle.

___ 6. Lot's wife, who was turned into a pillar of salt, was a granddaughter of Abraham.

___ 7. Absalom and Solomon were half-brothers.

___ 8. In Paul's second letter to Timothy, he mentions by name Timothy's mother, Lois, and his grandmother, Eunice.

___9. Mary, the mother of Jesus, had a father-in-law named Matthan (Joseph's father).

___10. Gideon had many wives and fathered seventy sons.

___11. As Rachel was dying, she gave birth to a son, Benjamin.

___12. Jethro, the priest of Midian, had a son-in-law named Moses.

___13. Jeremiah was forced to watch as his sons were killed before his eyes.

___14. Simon Peter and Andrew were brothers who were the first two apostles called by Jesus. He later nicknamed them "Sons of Thunder."

___15. The first two children mentioned in the Old Testament are Pebbles and Bam Bam.

___16. Other than being one of "the Israelites from the royal family and the nobility," Daniel (who wrote the book bearing his name) mentions no details of his family or relatives.

___17. Queen Esther had been raised by Mordecai, who was her cousin.

___18. Joseph son of Jacob had only one full brother, who was Benjamin.

___19. The father of disciples James and John approached Jesus and requested that his sons sit on Jesus' right and left in his coming kingdom.

___20. Mary, the mother of Jesus, and Elizabeth, the mother of John the Baptist, were related.

Relatively correct answers on page 202.

"Hello! Eve here again to congratulate you on making it through chapter five. You're pretty persistent! I just hope you've been playing by the rules. Believe me, I KNOW where that can get you.

"Thanks for coming along. Now I'm going to turn the stage over to a real world class Bible guy. Okay folks, it's the time you've been waiting for: the one and only MOSES!"

(Wild ovation, seas part, ground shakes, etc.)

"Oh, please, sit down everyone. After all, remember, I was a fairly reluctant leader. I tried just about every excuse to get God to consider choosing someone else to lead the people, but he ended up getting his way. (Seems like that happened a lot, for some reason.)

"By the way, I saw Noah backstage, and we were discussing how we both built arks. He obviously built a big one to float in, and I had the ark of the covenant built. Interestingly enough, mine held tablets, and Noah said they had tablets in their ark too . . . for seasickness!

MOSES GOES TO THE INTERNET FOR HELP
WITH DIRECTIONS.

"Anyway, since everybody seems to be tossing out their own 'top ten' lists, here's mine:

TOP TEN THINGS THAT FRUSTRATED ME (MOSES) ABOUT THE CHILDREN OF ISRAEL

10. Whenever they had Crackerjacks, they worshiped the little toys in the box
9. Constantly complained about the lack of good restroom facilities
8. Always tried to do fancy wind-ups when stoning
7. Had sung "100 bottles of wine on the wall" for twenty-eight years
6. Had lousy mannas
5. Kept telling me Charlton Heston was better looking
4. Constantly referred to me as "Mo"
3. Didn't know how to throw a civilized party
2. Wanted to speed up burnt offerings by using microwaves
1. Kept coming to me with phony maps showing Egypt as the promised land

"Well, you're halfway through this; consider yourself as having wandered in the wilderness for **twenty** years!

"I'll be back again at the end of chapter six!"

HITTING YOUR STRIDE
ANSWERS

Getting into the Act
Pages 167-168

1. True (2 Sam. 13:1–6)
2. False (Gen. 29:21–25)
3. True (1 Kings 20:37–38)
4. True (Matt. 22:15–19)
5. False (1 Sam. 28:8)
6. False (Gen. 12:10–20)
7. False (they were actually the "Porkettes" from Samaria City Music Hall)
8. True (1 Sam. 21:10–15)
9. False (Mark 6:14)
10. False (2 Sam. 14:1–24)
11. True (Gen. 27:6–41)
12. True (Josh. 9:3–16)
13. False (1 Kings 14:1–6)
14. False (Matt. 2:7–12)
15. True (2 Chron. 35:22)
16. True (1 Kings 22:30–37)

We Are Women
Pages 169-172

1. Vashti (Esther 1:10–12)
2. Damaris (Acts 17:34)
3. Miriam (Num. 12:1–16)
4. Merab (1 Sam. 18:17–19)
5. Joanna (Luke 8:3)
6. Abigail (1 Sam. 25:42; 1 Chron. 2:16)
7. Anna (Luke 2:36–38)
8. Cozbi (Num. 25:15)
9. Phoebe (Rom. 16:1)
10. Gomer (Hos. 1:1–3)
11. Keturah (Gen. 25:1–2)
12. Elizabeth (Luke 1:5–25, 57)
13. Rizpah (2 Sam. 3:7; 21:8–14)
14. Michal (1 Sam. 18:20–27)
15. Naomi (Ruth 1:19–21)

16. Candace (Acts 8:27)
17. Zeresh (Esther 5:10)
18. Dinah (Gen. 34:1–2)
19. Hannah (1 Sam. 1:12–16)
20. Jochebed (Exod. 6:20)
21. Mary (John 2:3)
22. Jezebel (2 Kings 9:30–37)
23. Mary Magdalene (Matt. 28:1)
24. Lois (2 Tim. 1:5)

It's A Living (Part Two)
Pages 173-177

1. B. (1 Chron. 26:7)
2. A. (Rom. 16:23)
3. D. (Gen. 21:20)
4. B. (Acts 16:14)
5. D. (Neh. 1:11)
6. A. (Gen. 4:2)
7. C. (Philem. 1:10–16)
8. C. (1 Chron. 11:6)
9. B. (Mark 6:3)
10. B. (1 Kings 21:1)
11. D. (Matt. 9:9)
12. A. (Gen. 16:1)
13. D. (Acts 23:24)
14. D. (1 Chron. 15:19)
15. A. (Gen. 4:22)
16. B. (Matt. 26:3)
17. A. (Judg. 6:11)
18. D. (Josh. 13:22)
19. D. (Acts 19:24)
20. C. (1 Sam. 14:50)
21. C. (1 Kings 16:31)
22. A. (Esther 1:10)

My Two Sons
Pages 179-180

1. Yes (Luke 15:12)
2. No (Luke 15:13)

3. No (Luke 15:14)
4. No (The "far country exclusion" eliminated him.)
5. Yes (Luke 15:15)
6. Yes (Luke 15:17–19)
7. No
8. No (Luke 15:20)
9. Yes (Luke 15:22)
10. No (Luke 15:23)
11. Yes (Luke 15:25–27)
12. No (Luke 15:28–32)
13. Yes (Luke 15:29)
14. No
15. Yes (Luke 15:30)
16. Yes (Luke 15:32)
17. No
18. No

Bonus: The dog's name was "Tramp."

May I Have This Dance?
Pages 181-183

1. David (2 Sam. 6:14–22)
2. Herodias's daughter (Mark 6:21–28)
3. wailing (Ps. 30:11)
4. Moses (Exod. 32:19)
5. the women of Israel (1 Sam. 18:6–7)
6. the prodigal son's older brother (Luke 15:25)
7. children (Matt. 11:16–17)
8. Jephthah (Judg. 11:34)
9. mourn (Eccles. 3:4)
10. Benjamin (Judg. 21:16–23)
11. Miriam (Exod. 15:20–21)
12. Job (Job 21:7–12)
13. the last two (149–150) (Pss. 149:3; 150:4)
14. Jeremiah (Jer. 31:4)

Hey, Good Lookin'
Pages 184-186

1. Vashti (Esther 1:9–12)
2. Absalom (2 Sam. 14:25)
3. Moses (Acts 7:20; Heb. 11:23; see also Exod. 2:2)
4. The Shulammite woman (Song of Sol. 1:5; 6:13)
5. Joseph (Gen. 39:6–20)
6. Abishag (1 Kings 1:1–4)
7. Tamar (2 Sam. 13:1–20)
8. Rachel (Gen. 29:17)
9. Samson (Judg. 15:2)
10. Bathsheba (2 Sam. 11:1–5)
11. Muhammed Ali
12. Esther (Esther 2:7)
13. Rebekah (Gen. 24:15–16)
14. Job (Job 42:15)
   (Author's note: That was supposed to be his **reward!** Go figure!)
15. Abigail (1 Sam. 25:3)
16. David (1 Sam. 16:12–13)
17. Sarai (Sarah) (Gen. 12:11–13; see also 20:2)
   A similar story (doublet) about Isaac and Rebekah appears in Genesis 26:7. However, the text does not specifically say that Isaac discussed the situation with Rebekah.

Second Wives Club
Pages 188-192

(Sorry, if you goof up the first time, you don't get a second chance here!)

1. C. (1 Sam. 25:42)
2. B. (Gen. 25:1)
3. B. (Gen. 4:19)
4. D. (Gen. 29:16–30)
5. A. (Num. 12:1)
6. D. (Rom. 7:1–3)
7. A. (Gen. 36:2–3)

8. C. (Ruth 4:10)
9. C, D. (1 Tim. 5:14)
10. E. (Judg. 14–16)
11. B. (1 Sam. 1:2)
12. D. (2 Sam. 14:27)
13. C. (1 Kings 3:1, 11:3)
14. B. (2 Kings 24:10–15)
15. A. (2 Chron. 11:18–21)
16. B. (Esther 1:12,19; 2:1–4)
17. D. (Hos. 1:3; 3:1–3)
18. C, E. (1 Tim. 3:1–2, 8, 12)

It's All Relative
Pages 193-195

1. False (Ruth 4:17)
2. True (Heb. 7:1–3)
3. True (John 11:1–2)
4. False (Gen. 5:21)
5. True (2 Kings 24:17)
6. False (Gen. 14:12)
7. True (2 Sam. 3:2–3; 12:24)
8. False (2 Tim. 1:5)
9. False (Matt. 1:15–16)
10. True (Judg. 8:30)
11. True (Gen. 35:18)
12. True (Exod. 3:1)
13. False (Jer. 52:10)
14. False (Mark 3:17)
15. False (although according to Ezekiel 3:9, the prophet had a forehead harder than flintstone)
16. True (Dan. 1:6)
17. False (Esther 2:7)
18. True (Gen. 43:29–34; 44:20)
19. False (Matt. 20:20–21)
20. True (Luke 1:36)

RUN LIKE THE WIND, BULLSEYE!

CAVES, GRAVES, KNAVES, SLAVES, & WAVES

(Eat your heart out, Robert Frost!)

All of the following questions fall in these five categories. Be on guard!

1. _____ found five enemy kings hiding in a cave at Makkedah. He killed them and entombed their bodies in the same cave.

2. Abraham and Sarah's grave was the cave of _____.

3. This "knave" (deceitful person) named _____ hoped to destroy the Jews, but his plan was foiled. He was hanged on a gallows which he had designed for the death of his worst enemy.

4. In the Epistle to Philemon, Paul focuses on returning a slave named _____.

5. When a tempest created life-threatening waves, the crew of the ship on which _____ was a passenger tossed him overboard.

6. According to the apostle John, after the opening of the _____ seal, the kings and mighty men "hid in caves and among the rocks of the mountains."

7. In his prophecy about the Messiah, _____ said, "He was assigned a grave with the wicked."

8. According to Matthew's account, when Judas came with the chief priests to arrest Jesus, Jesus addressed him saying, " _____, do what you came for."

9. _____ was sold as a slave to the Ishmaelites for twenty shekels of silver.

10. After being tempest tossed on the Adriatic Sea, Paul and 275 other persons ended up on the island of _____. (No, there was no Mr. and Mrs. Howell, no Ginger or Mary Ann.)

11. When David was hiding out in the cave of _____, his relatives came to see him.

12. While all four of the Gospels indicate Joseph of Arimathea prepared Jesus' body and laid it in a tomb, John states that Joseph was assisted by _____.

13. Their deceit included lying to the apostles about the proceeds of a sale of some property, and it cost _____ and _____ their lives.

14. The prophet Joel accuses the two cities of _____ and _____ of selling the people of Judah and Jerusalem as slaves to the Greeks.

15. _____ refers to false teachers, who "have taken the way of Cain," and "are wild waves of the sea, foaming up their shame."

16. When King Saul went into the cave at En Gedi to "relieve himself," David (who happened to be hiding in the recesses of the cave) _____ of Saul's robe.

17. According to Numbers 19:16, anyone who touches a grave would be unclean for _____ days.

18. This "knave" king was asked by his people to lighten their burden, but instead King _____ said, "My father made your yoke heavy; I will make it even heavier." (I guess he didn't want to be a good egg.)

19. If a man put out the eye or knocked out a tooth of his slave, the slave's compensation was _____.

20. God asked, "Where were you when I laid the earth's foundation?" and "when I said, 'This far you may come and no farther; here is where your proud waves halt'?" The **you** refers to _____.

On page 240 are the solutions every reader craves, for Caves, Graves, Knaves, Slaves, and Waves. (I hope this section is one of your faves.)

OUCH! (PART TWO)

(More unusual and/or painful ways to die)

   Match the unfortunate souls with their related method of demise.

Jezebel   Ahab
Goliath   two companies of 51 men
eldest son of Mesha,   Absalom
   king of Moab   Samson
Nadab & Abihu   Stephen
James Dean   Zimri & Cozbi
Haman   Abner
Joram   Zechariah
John the Baptist   an unnamed "man of God"
Ahaziah   Eglon
Hamor & Shechem   Ahithopel
"a certain Levite's"
   concubine

1. This person was shot between the shoulders with an arrow.

         Answer: _____

2. He was stabbed in the stomach by Joab.

         Answer: _____

3. They were burned alive, for disobedience.

         Answer: _____

4. He was stoned to death while Saul (Paul) stood by and approved.

         Answer: _____

5. She was tossed out a window, trampled, then eaten by dogs.

   Answer: _____

6. After being deceived by an unscrupulous prophet, he was killed by a lion.

   Answer: _____

7. He was struck by ten young men, while suspended from a tree by his head.

   Answer: _____

8. He was offered as a burnt sacrifice on a wall.

   Answer: _____

9. He put his "house in order" then committed suicide by hanging.

   Answer: _____

10. He was decapitated at the request of a young woman.

    Answer: _____

11. He was thrust through with a spear.

    Answer: _____

12. He died in an automobile accident.

    Answer: _____

13. He was killed with swords after being circumcised.

    Answer: _____

14. He was crushed to death by a falling building.

    Answer: _____

15. He was stoned to death in the court of the temple.

    Answer: _____

16. He died after a fall through the lattice of an upper room.

    Answer: _____

17. He died after a taking a direct hit in the head with a stone, hurled at him by a much smaller opponent.

    Answer: _____

18. He was hanged from an unusually tall gallows that he had built for someone else.

    Answer: _____

19. This "very fat" Moabite king was stabbed in the stomach by a left-handed man who carried a "foot-and-a-half-long" sword.

    Answer: _____

20. He was consumed by fire from heaven after a brief conversation with Elijah.

    Answer: _____

21. He was killed in battle by an arrow.

    Answer: _____

Now turn to page 240 for the answers—But for heaven's sake . . . Be Careful!

H2-OH, OH!

Water you doing here? Oh, I sea. **Well,** let me "pond"er this for a minute. Go with the flow and see how many of these "water" questions you can navigate. (Warning: Some of them may be hard to swallow.)

1. This body of water was to be the western border of the "promised land" (Canaan).

   A. The Nile River
   B. The Great Sea (Mediterranean)
   C. The Salt Sea (Dead Sea)
   D. Sea of Chinnereth (Galilee)
   E. Lake Tahoe

2. "I came into your house. You did not give me any water for my feet, but [this woman] wet my feet with her tears and wiped them with her hair." When Jesus said this, to whom was he speaking?

   A. Zachaeus
   B. Peter and John
   C. Pontius Pilate
   D. A Pharisee named Simon

3. In the last chapter of his book, Daniel sees two men on the opposite banks of the river. What is the one who is "above the waters of the river" wearing?

   A. Nothing
   B. A garment dipped in blood
   C. Linen
   D. A golden tunic
   E. Bell-bottomed slacks and a Nehru jacket

4. Water appears for the first time in the Bible in which of the following verses?

   A. Genesis 1:1
   B. Genesis 1:2
   C. Genesis 1:3
   D. Genesis 1:4
   E. Genesis 1:5

5. In Psalm 18, which does David say happened immediately before "the valleys of the sea were exposed, and the foundations of the earth laid bare"?

   A. The Lord shot his arrows and scattered the enemies
   B. God parted the ancient oceans with his words
   C. The waters of the deep churned relentlessly
   D. A tornado, after which a young girl's house landed on a wicked witch, caused a bunch of really short people to sing

6. In what body of water was John baptizing people at the beginning of the book of Mark?

   A. The Sea of Galilee
   B. The River Kishon
   C. A small lake near Samaria
   D. The Jordan River
   E. His Jacuzzi

7. Isaiah says, "The Lord will dry up the gulf of the _____ ."

   A. Egyptian Sea
   B. River Euphrates
   C. Salt Sea
   D. "Ancient river of Eden"
   E. Loch Ness monster

8. When the second trumpet sounds in Revelation 8, how much of the sea becomes blood?

   A. All of it
   B. One-half of it
   C. One-third of it
   D. Two-thirds of it

9. Solomon says in Proverbs 18 that "_____ are deep waters."

   A. The smiles of an evil woman
   B. The hidden ways of wisdom
   C. The words of a man's mouth
   D. The ways of righteous kings
   E. Places marked "Swim at your own risk"

10. What body of water did God part for the Israelites in Joshua 3?

    A. The Red Sea
    B. The Salt Sea
    C. The Sea of Chinnereth
    D. The Jordan River
    E. The water hazard on the sixth hole at Four Terebinths Golf Club

11. Through what prophet did God say, "See, I will make this people eat bitter food, and drink poisoned water"?

    A. Zephaniah
    B. Jeremiah
    C. Isaiah
    D. Ezekiel
    E. Micah

12. When Nahum said the Lord "rebukes the sea and dries it up; he makes the rivers run dry," he was preaching against

    A. Nineveh
    B. Babylon

C. Judah
D. Tyre and Sidon
E. Jet skis

13. "Whoever believes in me, as the Scripture has said, streams of living water will flow from within him." Where was Jesus when he said this?

A. The Mount of Olives
B. In the synagogue
C. At a Jewish feast
D. On the cross

14. In the book of Job, who used the analogy of water disappearing from the sea, and a river becoming parched and drying up, as being symbolic of human death?

A. Eliphaz
B. Zophar
C. Job
D. Bildad
E. Job's wife

15. After hearing an angel's voice from heaven, God showed her a well of water in the wilderness.

A. Mary
B. Hagar
C. Sarah
D. Rebekah

16. In Matthew 3, John the Baptist said, "I baptize you with water. . . . But after me will come one who is more powerful than I. . . . He will baptize you with _____."

A. Blood and suffering
B. Thunder and lightning

C. Living water and the Holy Spirit
D. The Holy Spirit and fire
E. None of the above

17. Which Bible writer referred to ungodly men as "clouds without rain"?

A. Moses
B. Jude
C. Paul
D. Peter
E. A meteorologist friend of Noah's who had predicted sunshine and drought for the next forty days

18. According to John's account, it is most likely that the body of water Jesus is said to have "walked" upon was

A. The Sea of Galilee
B. The lake called Gennesaret
C. The northern tip of the Salt Sea
D. Actually a part of the Jordan River

19. "Were you angry with the rivers, O Lord? Was your wrath against the streams? Did you rage against the sea when you rode with your horses and your victorious chariots?" Which minor prophet wrote these words?

A. Hosea
B. Haggai
C. Habakkuk
D. Malachi
E. Tony, "Little Prophet" Gambino

20. According to Psalm 104, what does the Lord "lay" "on their waters"?

A. The mighty creatures of the sea
B. The shadows of the great mountains

C. The vast foundations of his holy footstool

D. The beams of his upper chambers

21. According to Jesus' words in Matthew 10, "If anyone gives even a cup of cold water to one of these _____ because he is my _____ . . . he will certainly not lose his reward."

   A. Samaritans/follower
   B. Sinners/friend
   C. Strangers/worshiper
   D. Little ones/disciple
   E. Golfers/caddy

I hope these "H2-Oh, Oh" questions weren't over your head. Anyway, if you're fishing for answers, you'll hook 'em on page 241.

While we're on the subject of water, how about a list of the

TOP TEN REASONS ISAAC DUG WELLS IN THE VALLEY (GEN. 26:15–33)

10. He could never say no when someone asked, "Can you dig it?"
9. Figured he was better off with the well than the sick
8. Had an idea about marketing the water in a sports bottle
7. He was an expert at driving home a point
6. Water from the Red Sea made lousy Kool Aid
5. Cowboys needed to fill canteens
4. Was hoping to strike oil
3. Wanted to try out his solar powered submersible pump
2. Just part of his "wellness" program
1. Needed to make a wish

A CLEAN "WEEP"

"Knock knock!"
   "Who's there?"
   "Boo."
   "Boo who?"
   "Whaddaya cryin' about?!"
   Okay, okay . . . of course I heard it in the first grade. It just goes to show that you should never throw away an old joke. (Okay, maybe we should make some exceptions.)
   To assist you in determining the correct response to these questions about crying, I'm going to give you the correct amount of letters for the name or word. (Kinda like "Hangman." Looks like we're all going back to the first grade for a while!)

1. "But _ _ _ _ _ continued up the Mount of Olives, weeping as he went . . . and all the people with him . . . were weeping."

2. "Then _ _ _ _ answered and said, 'Why are you weeping and breaking my heart?'"

3. "There will be no more _ _ _ _ _, or mourning, or crying, or pain."

4. "Then _ _ _ _ _ _'s wife threw herself on him, sobbing, and said, 'You hate me! You don't really love me!'"

5. "_ _ _ _ _ , [who] . . . offered up prayers and petitions, with loud cries and tears to the one who could save him from death, and he was heard because of his reverent submission."

6. Jesus wept, over the death of his friend _ _ _ _ _ _.

7. "All night long I flood my bed with weeping and drench my _ _ _ _ _ with my tears."

8. "_ _ _ _ _ _ again pleaded with the king, falling at his feet and weeping. She begged him to put an end to the evil plan."

9. "But the subjects of the kingdom will be thrown outside, into the darkness. There will be weeping and _ _ _ _ _ _ _ _ of _ _ _ _ _."

10. When he heard about the condition of Jerusalem and the survivors of the captivity, _ _ _ _ _ _ _ _ "sat down and wept" and mourned for days.

11. Upon hearing from the prophet _ _ _ _ _ _ that he was about to die, Hezekiah prayed to the Lord and "wept bitterly."

12. After telling the mother of a dead man not to cry, Jesus touched the _ _ _ _ _ _ and commanded the man to "get up."

13. "Big Girls Don't Cry" was a big sixties hit for The _ _ _ _ _ _ _ _ _ _.

14. "A time to weep, and a time to _ _ _ _ _."

15. "While _ _ _ _ was praying, and confessing, weeping and throwing himself down before the house of God, a large crowd of Israelites—men, women and children—gathered around him. They too wept bitterly."

16. After Peter had denied Jesus the third time, he heard the sound of the _ _ _ _ _ _ _, and remembered what the Lord had told him. "Then he went outside and wept."

17. Paul's instructions to the Christians at Rome included " _ _ _ _ _ _ _ with those who _ _ _ _ _ _ _; mourn with those who mourn."

18. "When _ _ _ _ heard his father's words, he burst out with a loud and bitter cry."

19. "So I weep, as Jazer weeps, for the vines of _ _ _ _ _ _ ." (Good luck!)

20. "I wept and wept, because no one was found who was _ _ _ _ _ _ to open the _ _ _ _ _ _ or look inside."

Didn't get 'em all? Hey, it's nothing to cry about! The answers are right tear, oops, I mean right **here** on page 241! (Okay— read 'em and weep!)

COMMAND PERFORMANCE!

OOPS! It looks like Moses' secretary (who could be male **or** female) took a few naps while the boss was dictating the Ten Commandments for reprint to the masses. There are some corrections (**edits,** as we writers say) that must be made before Moses sends these to the printers. See if you can find the errors and make the necessary "repairs." (Note: a mistake may be a **significant** addition, omission, or inaccuracy. Good luck!)

1. I am the Lord your God, who brought you out of Israel, and out of the land of slavery. You shall hide no other gods behind me.

2. You shall not make for yourself an idol in the form of anything that is in heaven above, or on the earth beneath or in the waters below. You shall not bow down to them or worship them; you shall not place them at the Gates of Zion.

3. You shall not misuse the name of the Lord your God, for in the day that you take the Lord's name in vain, you will surely die.

4. Remember the Sabbath day, by keeping it holy. Five days you shall labor and do all your work. The sixth day is for watching cartoons and mowing the lawn, but on the seventh, you shall rest. On it you you shall not do any work, neither you, nor your son or daughter, nor your manservant or your maidservant. Only the uncircumcised stranger within your gates may toil on the Sabbath day.

5. Honor your father and mother, that their days may be long upon the land the Lord your God is giving you.

6. You shall not murder. An exception will be made for killing time.

7. You shall not commit adultery.

8. You shall not steal away to commit adultery.

9. You shall not witness falsely to a bear.

10. You shall not cover your neighbor's house, nor his wife, his servant, nor his car. Let him cover his own stuff.

11. You shall be careful about what you read. Be suspect of Bible trivia books. What these writers say shall never be written in stone.

Hmmm. Rather than rethinking the Ten Commandments, let's see where Moses' scribe missed the mark. (I wonder if they had "Chip Out" correction fluid for mistakes chiseled in stone! Or "Liquid Rock," maybe.)

Now thou shalt turn to page 242 for the answers, and thou shalt have a greater respect for editors!

JUST "WING" IT!

Halo again! Pull a cherub and sit down. Then see how well you do with these angel questions. Me? I just flew in from Chicago, and, boy, are my wings tired!

1. An angel of the Lord spoke to Philip and instructed him to go

    A. South toward Samaria
    B. South along the road to Gaza
    C. East on the Emmaus Road toward Jericho
    D. With Paul, to Thessalonica
    E. On a diet

2. An angel appeared to Jesus "and strengthened him" right after he

    A. Was brought before Pilate
    B. Cleared the money changers from the temple
    C. Walked on the sea
    D. Prayed on the Mount of Olives

3. This prophet had an angel bring a "live coal" to him, and touched it to the prophet's mouth!

    A. Isaiah
    B. Jeremiah
    C. Ezekiel
    D. Zechariah
    E. "Hot lips" Habakkuk

4. Jacob told of a dream he had about the angel of God, who called his attention to

    A. The coming of an Egyptian army
    B. The approaching death of his wife, Rachel
    C. The importance of circumcising his slaves
    D. His possessions, and a need to return to his father, Isaac

5. Acts 10 mentions a man named Cornelius who, in a vision, saw an angel. The angel instructed him to send for

   A. Saul
   B. Simon (Peter)
   C. Philip
   D. Luke
   E. His other brothers, and Sister Rose

6. The apostle John sees four angels standing at the four corners of the earth. What are they holding?

   A. Four diadems (crowns)
   B. Four seals
   C. The four winds
   D. Four trumpets
   E. A barbecue

7. All of the following people were told by an angel what to name their soon-to-be-born children, except one. Who?

   A. A daughter of Levi who was the mother of Moses
   B. Hagar, mother of Ishmael
   C. Zechariah, father of John the Baptist
   D. Mary, mother of Jesus

8. His life was saved when "the angel of the Lord" intervened just in time!

   A. Jacob
   B. Elisha
   C. Isaac
   D. Stephen
   E. None of the above

9. Which one of the following things did an angel of the Lord do for Peter?

   A. Healed his ear when it was severed by a sword during the arrest of Jesus
   B. Fed him from a giant sheet containing all kinds of animals, birds, and creeping things
   C. Allowed him to walk on the water to Jesus
   D. Busted him out of jail
   E. Bought Peter a "fish-finder" for his boat

10. An angel stood among the myrtle trees and showed him horses, a man with a measuring line, and Joshua, the high priest, being opposed by Satan. Who was this prophet?

   A. Zephaniah
   B. Nahum
   C. Malachi
   D. Zechariah
   E. Haggai

11. Not all angels in the Bible are good. Revelation 9:11 mentions this evil angel as "king . . . of the bottomless pit."

   A. Lucifer
   B. Abaddon
   C. Mephistopheles
   D. Beelzebub
   E. Molech

12. For what could be construed as blasphemy, this king was struck by an angel, leading to his demise.

   A. Herod
   B. Joash
   C. Agrippa
   D. Solomon
   E. Don King

13. When the angel wrestled with Jacob, he touched Jacob on the hip. What was the outcome of this?

   A. Jacob's leg was paralyzed for seven days
   B. Jacob's hip carried "the mark of God for all of his days"
   C. Jacob told the angel to bless him
   D. The angel renamed Jacob, "Israel"
   E. All of the above are true
   F. Only C and D are correct

14. What angel was instructed to help Daniel understand his vision concerning the ram, goat, and little horn?

   A. Michael the archangel
   B. The "Ancient of Days"
   C. Gabriel
   D. Apollyon
   E. Roma Downey

15. Matthew is the only Gospel that claims an angel did which of the following:

   A. Ministered to Jesus while he was on the cross
   B. Appeared to the disciples in the upper room immediately after Jesus' crucifixion
   C. Rolled away the stone which covered Jesus' tomb
   D. Tore the veil of the temple in two at the hour Jesus died

16. According to Jude, Michael the archangel argued with someone regarding the body of Moses. Who?

   A. Peter
   B. The devil
   C. Gabriel
   D. David
   E. The mortician at Jerusalem Funeral Home

17. Which angels did Jesus say always see the face of "my Father in heaven"?

    A. Those who resisted Satan's rebellion
    B. Those who watch over children
    C. The angels of the poor and downtrodden
    D. The "angels of mercy"
    E. Charlie's angels

18. When the men of Sodom came to Lot's house wanting to sexually assault his angelic guests, how did the angels stop them?

    A. They struck four men dead, and the rest fled
    B. They went out to the men, then struck them so that the perpetrators were unable to move
    C. The ground opened around the men, and swallowed them
    D. The angels struck them all blind
    E. They forced the men to get counseling

19. According to 2 Kings 19, how many Assyrian soldiers did the angel of the Lord kill in one night?

    A. 185,000
    B. 40,000
    C. 345,000
    D. 70,000
    E. None—angels are non-violent

20. While aboard a ship bound for Italy, an angel appeared to Paul in a dream. What two things did the angel tell him?

    A. That they must turn the ship around and sail back to Sidon
    B. That Paul must be brought before Caesar
    C. That half of the men on board would die
    D. That all of the men would survive

E. That all of the men should eat
F. That they would run aground on a small island, and be greeted by a man and woman named Mr. and Mrs. Howell

Hmmm. Acts 27, Paul, Mr. and Mrs. Howell . . .

Apostle Paul's Isle
(Yup, to the old familiar tune)

Just turn to Acts and you'll read a tale —
A tale of a man named Paul,
Who was a prisoner on a ship
To an Italian port of call.

They sailed over to Lycia,
On the first leg of the trip,
Then Julius checked Paul onto
An Alexandrian ship. (An Alexandrian ship.)

They had sailed slowly many days,
The wind was not their friend;
Deaf ears ignored Paul's warnings
Of the journey's nasty end.

When a headwind "like a tempest" came,
The ship was tossed about;
The crew went scurrying all around
And threw lots of stuff out.

But an angel said in a dream of Paul's,
"Your life is well secured;
No one on board will perish,
But I hope the ship's insured."
(Yes, I hope the ship's insured.)

The Adriatic took its toll
And the ship did not survive.
The reefs of Malta swallowed it,
But the men swam in alive.

The sailors caught a giant fish,
Fed its gill to all the men.
Then Paul took the fish and blessed it
And it grew its gill again.
(Yes, it grew its gill again.)

(Of course, then Malta was renamed "Gill-again"s
Island.)

Sorry for the interruption. Your angelic answers are on page 242.

TOP TEN THINGS THAT DIDN'T WORK WELL, IMMEDIATELY AFTER THE FLOOD

10. Sewer system
9. Cable TV
8. Copy machines
7. Lawnmowers
6. Subway system
5. Chain letters
4. Firecrackers
3. Kleenex
2. Zip codes
1. People not on the ark

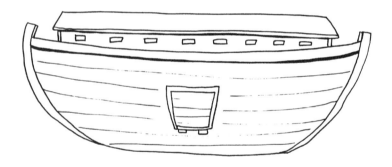

WAY TO GO, MO! (PART TWO)

And now we continue the story of Moses, a man whose kettle is always on the fire, yet he's never quite sure what he brews. (We're back to true/false!)

___ 1. After the Israelites left Egypt, Pharaoh decided to come after them with all the chariots of Egypt.

___ 2. Before God opened the Red Sea, the angel of God who went before the camp of Israel moved from the front to the rear of the camp.

___ 3. God parted the sea for Moses using a strong west wind, which blew the entire night.

___ 4. Just a few days after the miraculous crossing of the Red Sea, the people were already complaining about the lack of drinking water.

___ 5. The children of Israel were instructed to gather enough manna for everyone, and leave half of it to eat the following morning.

___ 6. During a battle against Amalek, Aaron's army fought for the Israelites while Joshua and Hur supported the arms of Moses to assure victory.

___ 7. Jethro, the father-in-law of Moses, convinced him to appoint judges over the people.

___ 8. Prior to giving the Ten Commandments, God told Moses that anyone who touched the mountain was to be put to death, either by stoning or being shot with an arrow.

___9. The final commandment God gave was regarding not coveting the property of a neighbor.

___10. After God gave the Ten Commandments to Moses, the people complained because they wanted God to speak directly to them.

___11. The Israelites were to refrain from plowing their fields every fifth year.

___12. The curtains over the tent of the tabernacle were to be made with the woven hair donated by seven young virgins.

___13. The Urim and Thummim were two items that were worn in the breast plate of Aaron when he entered the Holy Place.

___14. The Israelites were to be charged a fee during a census, and the charge was the same for the rich as for the poor.

___15. God threatened to destroy the Israelites for making a golden calf as an idol, but Moses asked God not to do it.

___16. Moses asked to see God's glory, but God said that no one could see his face and live.

___17. The Feast of Weeks was to be celebrated at the time the wheat was planted.

___18. The lampstand in the temple was made of fine silver and acacia wood.

___19. After the Tent of Meeting was completed, God instructed Moses to bring Joshua to the entrance, and anoint him with water.

___20. At one point, Moses could not enter the Tent of Meeting for a while because a cloud had settled upon it.

That's all the Mo we've got for now, but I have a feeling the pages may part for him again before your workout is over. So assemble your staff, and tell them the answers are on page 243.

THE ISRAELITES WERE A CONTINUAL SOURCE
OF CHALLENGE FOR MOSES.

CHURCH PLANTER'S PEANUTS

Like the elevator operator at the Washington Monument, Paul, the Bible's most celebrated church founder, had his share of ups and downs. And, as everyone who has ever been to church knows, the humans there can sometimes drive you nuts. Let's see if you can match the churches from this list with the descriptions below:

Macedonia   Philippi   Iconium   Ephesus
Lystra   Rome   Cyprus   Colosse   Galatia
Syria/Cilicia Corinth Thessalonica Antioch

1. At this church, Paul and Barnabas were "dedicated" to spread the gospel.

    Answer: _____

2. Here, Barnabas was called Zeus, and Paul was referred to as Hermes.

    Answer: _____

3. The people of this city were divided, some agreeing with the apostles, and others with the Jews.

    Answer: _____

4. In his letter to the people of this church, Paul referred to them as "foolish" and asked who had "bewitched" them.

    Answer: _____

5. In this city, Paul cast a spirit out of a young girl. He later praised the church founded here as being the only one who supported him in the "early days."

    Answer: _____

6. Bar-Jesus, also known as "Elymas the sorcerer," gave Paul some grief at this location.

    Answer: _____

7. Paul and his companions headed here after Paul dreamed that a man from this region was appealing for their help.

    Answer: _____

8. After a heated argument about John Mark, Paul parted company with Barnabas and took Silas to strengthen the churches here.

    Answer: _____

9. Paul sent a letter to the church here, but we don't know for sure if he ever visited this city.

    Answer: _____

10. Paul stayed here for a year and a half, working with Aquila, Priscilla, Titius, Justus, and Crispus.

    Answer: _____

11. Upon Paul's arrival here, he was guarded by a soldier. He rented a house here for two years.

    Answer: _____

12. Paul shaved his head just before coming here. He stayed briefly, left, then returned sometime later, and became involved in a dispute with a silversmith named Demetrius.

    Answer: _____

13. When the Jews of this city became upset with Paul's preaching, they took it out on his host, a man named Jason.

    Answer: _____

14. And now, to enhance your workout, a Brain-Strainer:

In his second letter to Timothy, Paul mentions three cities where he endured persecutions. All three appear in the above list, and you have used them each once (unless you messed up!). Give it a shot!
Answer: _____, _____, and _____

The well–established answers are located on page 244.

"Moses here again to congratulate you on conquering yet another chapter. If you're getting sick of this, let me hold up this serpent on a pole, and you can look at it and you'll feel— HEY—OUCH! The durned thing bit me! C'mon, you're a garter snake, you're supposed to snap, not bite!

"I'm leaving now to go get the snakebite kit, but here's someone I like to refer to as the 'Lion King'"—give it up for Daniel."

(Applause, applause!)

"Thanks, Mo—oops, I mean Moses. Actually, I'm a little embarrassed. I had something prepared, but I think I left it at home in the den. There's plenty of great stuff coming up in chapter seven, and I think you'll do just fine—the handwriting is already on the wall!

"Good luck—and I predict that you'll hear from me at the end of the next chapter!"

RUN LIKE THE WIND, BULLSEYE! ANSWERS

Caves, Graves . . .
Pages 205-207

1. Joshua (Josh. 10:16–27)
2. Machpelah (Gen. 25:9)
3. Haman (Esther 3:1–7:10)
4. Onesimus (Philem. 10–16)
5. Jonah (Jon. 1:11–15)
6. sixth (Rev. 6:12–15)
7. Isaiah (Isa. 53:9)
8. "Friend" (Matt. 26:50)
9. Joseph (Gen. 37:28)
10. Malta (Acts 27:41–28:1)
11. Adullam (1 Sam. 22:1)
12. Nicodemus (John 19:38–42)
13. Ananias/Sapphira (Acts 5:1–11)
14. Tyre/Sidon (Joel 3:4–6)
15. Jude (Jude 11–13)
16. cut off a corner (1 Sam. 24:1–4)
17. seven (Num. 19:16)
18. Rehoboam (1 Kings 12:14)
19. freedom (Exod. 21:26–27)
20. Job (Job 38:4, 11)

Ouch! (Part Two)
Pages 208-210

1. Joram (2 Kings 9:24)
2. Abner (2 Sam. 3:27)
3. Nadab/Abihu (Lev. 10:2)
4. Stephen (Acts 7:58; 8:1)
5. Jezebel (2 Kings 9:30–37)
6. An unnamed "man of God" (1 Kings 13:18–24)
7. Absalom (2 Sam. 18:9–15)
8. Eldest son of Mesha, King of Moab (2 Kings 3:27)
9. Ahithopel (2 Sam. 17:23)
10. John the Baptist (Matt. 14:1–12)
11. Zimri and Cozbi (Num. 25:7–8, 14–15)
12. James Dean
13. Hamor & Shechem (Gen. 34:13–26)

14. Samson (Judg. 16:30)
15. Zechariah (2 Chron. 24:20–22)
16. Ahaziah (2 Kings 1:2, 17)
17. Goliath (1 Sam. 17:49)
18. Haman (Esther 7:9–10)
19. Eglon (Judg. 3:16–22)
20. two companies of 51 men (2 Kings 1:9–12)
21. Ahab (1 Kings 22:34–37)

H2-Oh, Oh!
Pages 211-216

1. B. (Num. 34:6)
2. D. (Luke 7:36–47)
3. C. (Dan. 12:6)
4. B. (Gen. 1:2)
5. A. (Ps. 18:14–15)
6. D. (Mark 1:5)
7. A. (Isa. 11:15)
8. C. (Rev. 8:8)
9. C. (Prov. 18:4)
10. D. (Josh. 3:14–17)
11. B. (Jer. 9:15)
12. A. (Nah. 1:1–4)
13. C. (John 7:37–38)
14. C. (Job 14:11)
15. B. (Gen. 21:14–19)
16. D. (Matt. 3:11)
17. B. (Jude 12)
18. A. (John 6:1, 16–21)
19. C. (Hab. 3:8)
20. D. (Ps. 104:3)
21. D. (Matt. 10:42)

A Clean "Weep"
Pages 218-220

1. David (2 Sam. 15:30)
2. Paul (Acts 21:13)
3. death (Rev. 21:4)
4. Samson (Judg. 14:16)

5. Jesus (Heb. 5:6,7)
6. Lazarus (John 11:14, 35–36)
7. couch (Ps. 6:6)
8. Esther (Esther 8:3)
9. gnashing/teeth (Matt. 8:12)
10. Nehemiah (Neh. 1:1–4)
11. Isaiah (2 Kings 20:1–3)
12. coffin (Luke 7:13–14)
13. Four Seasons
14. laugh (Eccles. 3:4)
15. Ezra (Ezra 10:1)
16. rooster (Matt. 26:74–75)
17. rejoice (Rom. 12:15)
18. Esau (Gen. 27:34)
19. Sibmah (Isa. 16:9) (My undying respect if you knew this!)
20. worthy, scroll (Rev. 5:4)

Command Performance!
Pages 221-222

1. Israel should be Egypt; "No other gods before me" Exod. 20:2, 3
2. Added: "you shall not place them at the Gates of Zion" v. 4
3. Nothing about dying; will not be held "guiltless" v. 7
4. Added: lawn and cartoons; Strangers were not to work either vv. 9–10
5. Your days, not theirs v. 12
6. Added: killing time (Okay, okay, I know!) v. 13
7. Correct
8. Added "away to commit adultery" v. 15
9. (From KJV) "bear false witness" or "give false testimony against your neighbor" (NIV) v. 16
10. "covet" v. 17
11. ??

Just "Wing" It!
Pages 223-229

1. B. (Acts 8:26)
2. D. (Luke 22:39–43)
3. A. (Isa. 6:6–7)

4. D. (Gen. 31:11–13)
5. B. (Acts 10:1–5)
6. C. (Rev. 7:1)
7. A. (Exod. 2:1–10)
   (Gen. 16:1–12) (Hagar)
   (Luke 1:5–13) (Zechariah)
   (Luke 1:26–33) (Mary)
8. C. (Gen. 22:9–13)
9. D. (Acts 12:3–10)
10. D. (Zech. 1:8–9; 2:1–3; 3:1)
11. B. (Rev. 9:11)
12. A. (Acts 12:21–23)
13. F. (Gen. 32:24–32)
14. C. (Dan. 8:16)
15. C. (Matt. 28:1–2)
16. B. (Jude 9)
17. B. (Matt. 18:10)
18. D. (Gen. 19:1–11)
19. A. (2 Kings 19:35)
20. B, D. (Acts 27:24)

Way To Go, Mo! (Part Two)
Pages 231-233

1. True (Exod. 14:7)
2. True (Exod. 14:19)
3. False (Exod. 14:21)
4. True (Exod. 15:22–24)
5. False (Exod. 16:19)
6. False (Exod. 17:8–13)
7. True (Exod. 18:12–26)
8. True (Exod. 19:12–13)
9. True (Exod. 20:17)
10. False (Exod. 20:19)
11. False (Exod. 23:10–11)
12. False (Exod. 26:7)
13. True (Exod. 28:29–30)
14. True (Exod. 30:11–16)
15. True (Exod. 32:9–14)

16. True (Exod. 33:20)
17. False (Exod. 34:22)
18. False (Exod. 37:17)
19. False (Exod. 40:12)
20. True (Exod. 40:34–35)

Church Planter's Peanuts
Pages 234-237

1. Antioch (Acts 13:1–3)
2. Lystra (Acts 14:11–12)
3. Iconium (Acts 14:4)
4. Galatia (Gal. 3:1)
5. Philippi (Acts 16:16–18; Phil. 4:15)
6. Salamis (Acts 13:4–6)
7. Macedonia (Acts 16:9–10)
8. Syria, Cilicia (Acts 15:39–41)
9. Colosse (Col. 1:2; 2:1)
10. Corinth (Acts 18:1–3, 7–11)
11. Rome (Acts 28:16, 30)
12. Ephesus (Acts 18:18–21; 19:1, 23–41)
13. Thessalonica (Acts 17:5–9)
14. Antioch, Iconium, Lystra (2 Tim. 3:11)

KICKING IN THE AFTERBURNERS

(That means show me some **intensity!**)

A HAIRY START

The following multiple choice questions all relate to hair. See if you can brush through them with style.

1. Which of the following statements best represents the biblical account of Samson's hair?

    A. When Samson was a young boy, an angel appeared to him and instructed him not to cut his hair

    B. An angel appeared to Samson's mother and told her that she would have a son, and must never let anyone shave his head

    C. At age thirteen, Samson was circumcised by Abdon, and took a vow to never cut his hair

    D. When Samson became a Nazarite as a young adult, the requirement forbade him from ever cutting his hair again

    E. Samson let his hair grow after seeing the Beatles on The Ed Sullivan Show

2. Paul wrote to the Corinthian Christians that if a man has long hair, it is

    A. An abomination to God

    B. Glory to him

    C. A "stumbling block" to the weaker brother

    D. A disgrace

3. In Leviticus 19, Moses prohibits Hebrew men from trimming

    A. The edges of their beards, and the hair on the sides of their head

    B. Their facial hair

C. Any hair that grows from the body
D. The hair of their wives
E. The sails of their catamarans

4. Luke tells the story of a woman who washed Jesus' feet with her tears, and dried them with her hair. Where did this occur?

   A. In the temple at Jerusalem
   B. At the house of a Pharisee
   C. By the Sea of Galilee
   D. At the funeral of Lazarus

5. Proverbs 16:31 states that gray hair is

   A. Worthy of the respect of nations
   B. As an uncut diamond
   C. A crown of splendor
   D. A garland of wisdom
   E. Unavoidable if you have kids

6. In his first letter to Timothy, Paul suggests women should not do what to their hair?

   A. Braid it
   B. Cut it
   C. Cover it
   D. Color (dye) it
   E. Tease it

7. Absalom cut his hair when it became too heavy for him. The Bible says after he cut it, he

   A. Traded it to the soothsayers for gold
   B. Gave locks of it to his female admirers
   C. Blessed it, and threw it to the wind
   D. Weighed it

8. Isaiah says that the Lord will use this person as "a razor" to shave the heads, legs, and beards of Israelite men.

   A. Satan
   B. Cyrus, king of Persia
   C. The king of Assyria
   D. King Uzziah
   E. A sharp writer

9. Jesus told his disciples that the hairs on their heads were

   A. Insignificant to the Father
   B. Numbered
   C. Turning gray and dying
   D. Reborn in the resurrection

10. Job's friend Eliphaz the Temanite told of having the hair on his body stand on end because of fear. What scared him?

    A. A robber who threatened to kill him
    B. A spirit that passed in front of him
    C. The news of Satan's assault on Job's family
    D. A vision of skeletons in a valley
    E. A margin call from his broker

11. Why did the author of Ezra say that he tore his clothes and plucked hair from his head and beard?

    A. Because the Israelites had intermarried with non-Jewish peoples
    B. Because he heard that King Darius had sent soldiers to kill him
    C. Because the Israelites seemed uninterested in rebuilding the temple at Jerusalem
    D. Because the priests had failed to celebrate Passover, as commanded by Moses

12. The Lover in Song of Songs comments that his bride's hair is like a flock of goats descending a mountain. In chapter five, how does she describe his hair?

    A. "As beautiful as the hair of Absalom"
    B. "Like a crown, holy and regal"
    C. "Golden, and shining like the everlasting sun"
    D. "Wavy and black as a raven"
    E. "Kinda like Michael Jordan's"

13. According to Ezekiel, the Sovereign Lord says that these people were to keep their hair trimmed, neither shaving their heads nor letting it grow too long. To whom does this refer?

    A. The priests
    B. All the men of Israel
    C. Women
    D. Foreigners and slaves
    E. Soldiers

14. Paul's first letter to the Corinthians says that if a woman prays with her head uncovered, she dishonors

    A. The Holy Spirit
    B. Her husband
    C. Her head
    D. The resurrected Christ

15. Moses said that if an attractive woman was taken as a captive of war, she could be kept as a wife. What was mentioned about her hair?

    A. Her hair must not be cut
    B. She should shave her head
    C. Her hair was to be braided to distinguish her as a captured woman
    D. Her hair should be washed daily for seven days, as a rite of purification
    E. Her hair should be covered, or hidden, for a full month

16. After some youths mocked Elisha about his baldness, he placed a curse on them. What happened next?

   A. The youths were struck blind

   B. The youths were struck by lightning

   C. The youths apologized

   D. The youths were mauled by bears

   E. David showed up with a very large sling, looked straight at the youths, and said, "Go ahead, punks—make my day."

Well, you've made it though another hair-raising part of the workout. Let's harry on—oops, I mean **hurry** on to the answers on page 278.

Sequels have become a part of our tradition. Like **Star Wars, Jurassic Park, Back to the Future,** and even **Billy Jack** (oh oh, I'm starting to date myself), it seems like everyone's getting in on the act. So, why should we be any different? Here's the sequel to "Where Ya Been, Stranger?" from chapter two. Just match the person with the place they're most often associated with. There'll be another Top Ten list waiting when you're finished. (So much for incentive!)

Good luck!

WHERE YA BEEN, STRANGER? . . . THE SEQUEL

Places

Ephesus	Nazareth	Land of Benjamin	Assyria
Jericho	Canaan	North Pole	desert
Shiloh	Syria	Shechem	Egypt (used twice)
Uz	Eden	Moab	Babylon

1. _____ Neco

2. _____ Abraham

3. _____ Demetrius

4. _____ Job

5. _____ Sennacherib

6. _____ Santa Claus

7. _____ Adam & Eve

8. _____ Jesus

9. _____ Nehemiah

10. _____ Joseph (the coat guy!)

11. _____ John the Baptist

12. _____ Hannah

13. _____ Jeroboam

14. _____ Ben-Hadad

15. _____ Mesha (another easy one!)

16. _____ Jeremiah

17. _____ Nebuchadnezzar

There now, that wasn't so good, was it?! This isn't called **The Great Bible Trivia Workout** for nothing! The answers are on page 278.

And now, as promised, here is a list of the

TOP TEN THINGS DELILAH DIDN'T REALIZE WOULD DESTROY SAMSON'S STRENGTH

10. Cutting his jugular vein
9. Painting him red, calling him "Elmo," and then tickling him
8. "Brady Bunch" reruns
7. Taking away his steroids
6. Canceling his health club membership
5. Hiding his spinach
4. Reading poetry to him
3. A head cold
2. Plugging him into 220 volts
1. Shampoo

PETER BECOMES THE FIRST XTREME
SPORTS ENTHUSIAST

AIN'T MISBEHAVIN'

The following true/false questions all involve acts of obedience or disobedience. Now do as I say: make like a decal and apply yourself!

___ 1. After the angel released them from prison, the apostles were apprehended and brought before the Sanhedrin. It was then that Paul said, "We must obey God rather than men."

___ 2. Isaac commanded his son Jacob not to marry a Canaanite woman, but Jacob later disobeyed.

___ 3. Paul begins the sixth chapter of Ephesians by instructing, "Men, obey God."

___ 4. Samuel was disappointed that he had made Saul king because Saul often disobeyed Samuel's orders.

___ 5. Peter encouraged Christians to obey all human authorities.

___ 6. In the ninth year of King Hoshea, the Assyrians captured and deported Israel to Assyria. The writer claims this happened even though the children of Israel had been "obedient to God and his laws."

___ 7. Paul told the Galatian believers that he had boasted about their obedience to Titus.

___ 8. James says that horses naturally obey their riders, and our obedience to God should be the same.

___9. When the Lord told the prophet Elijah to head east of the Jordan, where he would drink from a brook and be fed by ravens, Elijah immediately complied.

___10. When God confronted Adam and Eve about eating the forbidden fruit, Adam blamed Eve, Eve blamed the serpent, and the serpent blamed a guy named Lenny.

___11. Jonah's disobedience to God led to his being thrown into the sea by a ship's crew, and then swallowed by a great fish.

___12. Peter speaks of disobedient spirits who apparently had been imprisoned since the days of Noah.

___13. Paul told the Thessalonians that God would punish those who were disobedient to the gospel of Jesus Christ until they repented.

___14. The writer of Hebrews encourages obedience to leaders so their work is joyful, not burdensome.

___15. When Moses and Aaron instructed the Hebrews about what they must do to avoid the final plague on Egypt (death of firstborn), as usual the people disobeyed.

___16. Because of their disobedience, God said that none of the Israelites of that generation would set foot in the promised land, except Moses and Joshua.

___17. Paul told the Romans that he had been a minister of Jesus Christ in bringing Gentiles to obedience of God.

Well, it looks like **you've** been obedient in doing your best on these questions, so I'm going to hold off on the fire and brimstone—at least temporarily! Here are the answers on page 279.

HAVE A NICE TRIP!

Bible characters were mobile. No, they didn't have e-tickets or frequent-flier miles, but they still managed to get around. The following questions are fill-in-the-blank, but to give you a break, we're just going to ask for the person or the location (town, country, etc.). You'll do just fine—now you better hurry, or you'll miss your . . . camel!

1. An angel appeared to Joseph in a dream, telling him to take Mary and the child Jesus and escape to _____.

2. _____ was seventy-five years old when God told him to leave his country and his people and set out from Haran.

3. Paul told the Thessalonians that when Satan hindered him from traveling to see them again, he sent _____ instead.

4. In the parable of the Good Samaritan, the man in the story who was attacked by thieves was traveling from Jerusalem to _____.

5. When instructed by God to go to Nineveh, _____ headed instead for Tarshish.

6. Upon hearing that Jerusalem was lying in shambles, _____ asked his boss, the king of Persia, for permission to go there and rebuild the city.

7. The book of Daniel begins with troops who traveled from _____ besieging Jerusalem.

8. Paul and his traveling companions left the city of _____ following the Feast of Unleavened Bread, then went to Troas for seven days.

9. _____ warned the believers about planning to travel to this city or that city, make a profit, and then return.

10. _____ received an all-expenses-paid trip to Egypt. Unfortunately, he went as a slave.

11. Samson and his parents were headed down to _____ to secure a wife for him when Samson killed a lion with his bare hands.

12. When Abraham and Lot parted ways, Abraham lived in Canaan, but Lot headed east toward _____.

13. After a severe famine, _____ left Moab and walked for many days back to Bethlehem.

14. According to Mark, after John the Baptist was imprisoned, Jesus went to _____ to begin his public ministry.

15. After having his life threatened by Jezebel, _____ hit the road, leaving his servant in Beersheba, then heading into the desert.

Now that we've made it home, it's time to put the camel in the garage, and unpack the trunk (Wait a minute, where did the elephant come from?). Maestro, a little traveling music to take us to the answers on page 279.

LOT'S TO THINK ABOUT

I've always found Lot's life to be an interesting study. Not that I've spent a lot of time on it, but as a writer of Bible trivia books (which is my lot in life), it just seems that he turns up a lot. So cast your lots with me and arrange these parts of the biblical account of "ole what's his name" in the proper chronological order. Simply put a #1 by the first event, a #2 by the second one, etc. Once you get started, don't look back. Lots of luck!

_____A. Lot's wife becomes a pillar of salt (not to be confused with a "pillar of the church").

_____B. Abram and Lot decide to separate.

_____C. Abraham talks with God about the possibility of not destroying Sodom.

_____D. Lot offers his virgin daughters to the corrupt men of Sodom.

_____E. Lot is captured by four attacking kings.

_____F. The angels give Lot permission to stop at Zoar, and he arrives there safely.

_____G. Lot unknowingly commits incest with his daughters.

_____H. The angels tell Lot to flee the city with his family.

_____I. The two angels arrive at Sodom, and Lot bows to them.

_____J. Lot's daughters give birth to sons.

_____K. Abram, his wife, and Lot leave Egypt.

_____ L. Lot and his daughters leave Zoar and move to a cave in the mountains.

_____ M. Lot heads east and settles near Sodom.

_____ N. Lot is rescued by Abram and his men.

_____ O. The men of Sodom are struck blind.

_____ P. The angels physically lead Lot's family out of the city.

I can only hope you got a lot of these correct. (Okay, no more punishment.) As set out in Genesis 13–19, the correct sequence is on page 280.

As a special "bonus lot" here are the:

TOP TEN REASONS LOT'S WIFE LOOKED BACK

10. To see if she'd rolled up the car windows
9. Knew it was the only way she'd ever get a statue of herself
8. Was certain she'd missed a garage sale
7. Iodine deficiency
6. Didn't mean to, but had a neck spasm
5. Wanted one last look at the mall
4. Saw Helen Hunt do it in "Twister"
3. Thought they said "fire and Flintstones"
2. Lot tricked her by throwing his voice behind her
1. It was a publicity stunt for Morton

YOU CAN'T EAT *THAT!*

It's a long time ago, and you are hungry. And boy, does that three-legged mongo look good to you. So good, in fact, that you could almost eat it raw! But wait . . . there are **rules** about such things.

The following multiple choice questions pertain to biblical culinary etiquette (that's putting it mildly). Bon appetit!

1. This part of an animal found dead could be used for any purpose except eating

   A. The tail
   B. The blood
   C. The hide, or outer skin
   D. The fat

2. When it is red, you should not consume it, lest it attack you like a snake!

   A. Meat from cattle
   B. Wine
   C. Goat's blood
   D. Manna
   E. Strawberry jello

3. According to Acts 21, Gentile believers were instructed to avoid eating all of the following except

   A. Meat of split-hooved animals
   B. Food sacrificed to idols
   C. Blood
   D. Meat of strangled animals

4. What was the penalty for eating the fat of an animal which is used for a fire offering to the Lord?

   A. Death by stoning
   B. A seven-day purification away from the camp

C. The family's best ram or goat would be confiscated
D. Being cut off from the people
E. The violator's microwave would be unplugged for a month

5. Joseph was asked by the Pharaoh of Egypt to interpret his dream, which concerned animals cannibalizing their own kind. What animals were they?

A. Pigs
B. Cows
C. Camels
D. Lions

6. Exodus 22 says that the people of God are not to eat the meat of an animal that has been torn by wild beasts. What are they instructed to do with it instead?

A. Bury it far from camp
B. Feed it to the foreigners and slaves
C. Throw it to the dogs
D. Cast it into the river

7. The Hebrews are reminded often not to consume the blood of animals or birds. Deuteronomy 12:23 offers a reason for this. What is it?

A. "The blood will surely choke you"
B. "Salvation comes by the blood, therefore blood is holy"
C. "The blood is the life, and you must not eat the life with the meat"
D. "The blood of an animal has been debased by God, as God has given man dominion over animals"
E. "Animal blood is B negative, and you people complain enough as it is"

8. When Paul discusses eating food that has been offered to idols, which of the following best summarizes his conclusion?

   A. Food does not bring us near to God
   B. Don't worry too much about what others think
   C. Stigmatized meat can defile even the purest believer
   D. The dietary laws of Moses no longer need to be followed
   E. Don't make any idols of Ronald McDonald

9. Whom was to receive the right thigh of a fellowship offering?

   A. The Lord
   B. Moses
   C. The man who brought the offering
   D. The descendant of Aaron

10. The Lord told Aaron that he and his sons were not to consume this inside the Tent of Meeting or they would die. What?

    A. Blood
    B. Wine or other fermented drink
    C. The fat of a sacrifice to him
    D. The meat of any sin offering

11. According to Deuteronomy 14, what type of "water creatures" were not to be eaten?

    A. Those that were of a length greater than one cubit (about eighteen inches)
    B. Eels and snakes
    C. Those creatures without fins and scales
    D. Those creatures with fins and scales
    E. There were no rules regarding water creatures

12. In the Sermon on the Mount, what did Jesus say about food?

    A. Whoever eats meat offered to idols is in danger of hell fire
    B. The lust to fill the stomach is a cause of many evils
    C. Eat, drink, and be merry—God wants everyone to be filled
    D. Don't worry about food because God knows your needs
    E. I can't preach on an empty stomach

13. Which of the following is not mentioned in the list of birds which were unlawful to eat?

    A. The falcon
    B. The dove
    C. The eagle
    D. The bat

14. What was the name of the tree in the Garden of Eden that held the forbidden fruit?

    A. The tree of the knowledge of good and evil
    B. The tree of life
    C. The tree of wisdom
    D. The fig tree
    E. The "Where Are Our Clothes?" tree

15. When Jesus was criticized for eating heads of grain on the Sabbath, he mentioned an Old Testament leader who once ate bread that was lawful only for priests to eat. Name him.

    A. David
    B. Moses
    C. Solomon
    D. Joshua

16. Choose the animal that was not to be eaten:

    A. Gazelle
    B. Ox
    C. Rabbit
    D. Antelope

17. While tempting Jesus in the wilderness, the devil appealed to Jesus' hunger by

    A. Offering him food prohibited by Moses
    B. Suggesting he turn stones into bread
    C. Encouraging Jesus to call angels to bring him food
    D. Making an offer to give Jesus food fit for a king, if Jesus would worship him
    E. Agreeing to split the cost of a Little Caesar's pizza

18. Regarding the eating of insects, Moses said

    A. Nothing
    B. All insects are lawful to eat
    C. No insects are to be eaten
    D. Flying insects that swarm are unclean
    E. Don't eat any insect that has been sprayed with Raid

Wow! All of this talk about food has certainly made me hungry! I wonder how Moses would have felt about Reese's Peanut Butter Cups—okay, maybe the chocolate and peanut butter would have been acceptable, but the orange wrapper, now that's a different matter entirely. Feel free to devour the answers—they're ready for consumption on page 280.

"SORRY ABOUT THAT, CHIEF!"

As a kid (which I once **was**), I always got a kick out of Maxwell Smart on the old spy spoof called **Get Smart**. In honor of Max, 99, the Chief, and good old-fashioned funny (and CLEAN) television, I dedicate this true/false section of your workout. All of the questions involve sorrow and apologies. If you accept this mission, you'll be risking your life every minute . . . and loving it!

___ 1.   Before Jonah was thrown into the sea, he apologized to the sailors for putting them in peril.

___ 2.   Afraid that his brother Esau would try to kill him, Jacob ran and bowed seven times as Esau approached with his men.

___ 3.   Although King Herod may have been sorry he offered to grant a request from Herodias's daughter, he still delivered on her demand and ordered John the Baptist beheaded.

___ 4.   According to the sixth chapter of Genesis, with the exception of Moses, the world was full of evil men; and God was sorry he'd created them.

___ 5.   Paul says in Romans 9 that he has great sorrow in his heart for his own race, the people of Israel.

___ 6.   Luke's account of the disciples sleeping while Jesus prayed at the Mount of Olives says that they were exhausted from sorrow.

___ 7.   After David cut off a piece of Saul's robe without his knowledge, David was sorry and apologized to Saul. Saul, however, responded angrily and threatened to kill David.

___8. In Ecclesiastes 7, the writer says that laughter is better than sorrow because "a cheerful face is good for the heart."

___9. The writer of Revelation saw God wiping tears and removing sorrow from the people by the River of Life just prior to the author seeing the new Jerusalem.

___10. While John 3:16 is probably the most quoted verse in the Bible, Genesis 3:16 talks about the pain in childbirth that women bear because Eve disobeyed God.

___11. When King David called upon God for mercy in Psalm 51, he was apologizing for his sin of adultery with Bathsheba.

___12. Isaiah, who was known as the "weeping prophet," was so sorrowful over the fall of Israel that he wrote a second book called Lamentations.

___13. When Judas became filled with remorse over betraying Jesus, he returned the thirty pieces of silver to the temple.

___14. When King David sent a delegation of messengers to express his sympathy over the death of the king of Ammon, the Ammonites accused the men of being spies and humiliated them.

___15. When Job's three friends came to visit, they barely recognized him, and immediately began crying and tearing their clothes in sympathy.

___16. After Shadrach, Meshach, and Abednego emerged from the fiery furnace unharmed, King Nebuchadnezzar begged their forgiveness, fearing that their God might kill him.

Well, are you sorry you attempted this section? Sorry, no refunds! Ha ha ha! We now will discover how sorry you really are . . . for the answers await on page 281.

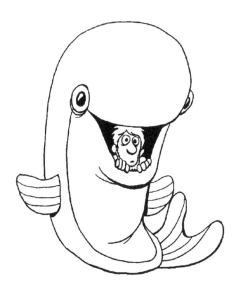

I SEE ... DEAD PEOPLE!

The Bible offers many instances of "unique" situations involving those who had, shall we say, "bought the farm." (Okay, so maybe that's not the **best** way to say it, but you get the idea.) I know you're simply dying to fill in the blanks, so go to it, you lucky stiff!

1. Only in the Gospel of _____ does the Bible mention that many dead people came back to life after Jesus' death on the cross.

2. The Lord told _____, "Your brother's blood cries out to me from the ground!"

3. Jesus was mocked just prior to raising the daughter of _____ from the dead.

4. According to Jude, a dispute took place between Michael the Archangel and the devil concerning the body of _____.

5. A long-winded sermon from Paul put _____ to sleep. He then fell from a third-story window, where his lifeless body was raised by Paul. (Paul almost became a pall-bearer.)

   A talkative preacher was Paul,
   Steadfast and true to the call —
   If occasionally boring
   He set someone snoring,
   Then they, and not he, took the fall.

6. Abraham bought the cave of Machpelah from _____ so that he would have a place to bury Sarah.

(If you know this one, you are something! I'm not sure what, but something!)

7. In Revelation 11, two prophets are apparently killed by "the beast . . . from the Abyss," and their bodies lie in the street of a city. The city is given two symbolic names of real places mentioned in the Bible. Feeling lucky? _____ and _____.

8. _____ was tossed out of a window, and when the men came to bury the corpse, all they found was a skull, feet, and hands.

9. After the crucifixion of Jesus, Matthew says that a rich man named _____ of _____ went to Pilate and requested the body, and was given it.

10. _____ held the body of his father, and wept over it; then he ordered the physicians under his leadership to embalm it.

11. Jeremiah tells the story of _____, son of _____, who killed eighty men and threw their bodies into a cistern. (Another toughie!)

12. _____ was led by the Spirit of the Lord into a valley of skeletons, which became corpses, then came to life. (Dem bones, dem bones, dem dry bones!)

13. Jesus cast a demon from a young boy, who appeared so corpse-like that he was assumed dead. After he rose, the disciples, who previously had failed to heal him, questioned Jesus about it. He replied that this type of exorcism required _____.

14. _____ was commanded by the Lord not to marry and have children where he lived; for if he did, his family would die of deadly diseases and their bodies would be food for birds and beasts.

15. Although the father of _____ had offered kindness to King Joash, the king still authorized this man's stoning in the temple courtyard. As he was dying, he called upon the Lord for justice.

16. At Endor, King Saul sought a medium who raised the spirit of _____.

Are you glad it's over? It is for all of those people too! Ha ha! Get it? Okay, let's breathe some life back into you by going over the answers on page 281.

"OLDEN GOLDIES"

From King Midas to Goldfinger, the allure of the yellow metal has been powerful as long as humans have walked the planet. The Bible offers plenty of its own examples. Take your best shot at this matching quiz, and if you do well, you might just win a medal. Of course, it will be a **paper** medal! (Why not a new slogan: "Go for the paper!" Parakeets have done this for years.)

_____1. This royal's dream featured a statue with a golden head.

_____2. Good gold is here, where the Pishon River flows.

_____3. He wrote to the church that genuine faith was worth more than gold.

_____4. He compared a word well-spoken to "apples of gold."

_____5. As a child, he was given gold as a gift.

_____6. God instructed Moses to have garments of blue, purple, and scarlet yarn, and gold, made for this man and his sons.

_____7. This goldsmith was ordained by God to carry out the work of constructing the sanctuary.

_____8. This guest of Solomon's gave him 120 talents of gold—more than four tons! (I must have the wrong friends.)

_____9. A "gold cup in the LORD's hand."

_____10. He told his listeners that he would endure and "come forth as gold."

_____11. In his letter to this friend, Paul used gold to symbolize noble deeds.

_____12. He went bankrupt after gold-seekers destroyed his California mill in the 1850s.

A. Bezalel
B. Babylon
C. Timothy
D. Havilah
E. Nebuchadnezzar
F. Job
G. Peter
H. Jesus
I. Sutter
J. Aaron
K. Queen of Sheba
L. Solomon

When it comes to gold, I'm from the "hard knocks" versus "Fort Knox" department. Anyway, your 24-carat (or is that carrot?) answers glisten on page 282.

"Daniel here again! Like I said, you did just fine, right? Right? Well, no one's perfect. Anyway, I've interpreted your dreams (except the one where you're walking down the street in your underwear), and I'm staying with my original prophecy: you'll complete this book before the world comes to an end.

"Now, to lead you into chapter eight, here's an old pal of mine who could bench press five Philistines . . . and that was before he **really** let his hair down! How about a big hand for . . . Samson!"

(Yayyy, Hurrah, Hip Hip, Leg, Arm, Bicep!)

"Thanks, folks! I'm pretty pumped about being in this here Bible workout, and I happen to know this next chapter is a real honey, and I ain't lyin'. (Hmmm, sounds like a riddle I once made up.)

"Well, I gotta go thump on some Philistines, but I want you to really bring down the house this time. I'll keep an eye out for ya at the end of the line."

A Hairy Start
Pages 247-251

1. B. (Judg. 13:3–5)
2. D. (1 Cor. 11:14)
3. A. (Lev. 19:27)
4. B. (Luke 7:36–38)
5. C. (Prov. 16:31)
6. A. (1 Tim. 2:9)
7. D. (2 Sam. 14:26)
8. C. (Isa. 7:20)
9. B. (Matt. 10:30)
10. B. (Job 4:15)
11. A. (Ezra 9:1–3)
12. D. (Song of Sol. 4:1; 5:11)
13. A. (Ezek. 44:20)
14. C. (1 Cor. 11:5)
15. B. (Deut. 21:12)
16. D. (2 Kings 2:23–24)

Where Ya Been, Stranger?
Pages 252-253

1. Egypt (2 Chron. 35:20)
2. Canaan (Gen. 12:6–7; 13:12)
3. Ephesus (Acts 19:23–27)
4. Uz (Job 1:1)
5. Assyria (2 Kings 18:13)
6. North Pole (my mom)
7. Eden (Gen. 2:8)
8. Nazareth (Acts 2:22)
9. Jerusalem (Neh. 2:11)
10. Egypt (Gen. 37:28)
11. desert (Luke 1:80)
12. Shiloh (1 Sam. 1:1–5)
13. Shechem (1 Kings 12:25)
14. Aram (1 Kings 20:1)
15. Moab (2 Kings 3:4)
16. Land of Benjamin (Jer. 1:1)
17. Babylon (2 Kings 24:1)

Ain't Misbehavin'
Pages 255-256

1. False (Acts 5:27–29)
2. False (Gen. 28:1, 7)
3. False (Eph. 6:1)
4. False (1 Sam. 15:11)
5. True (1 Pet. 2:13–14)
6. False (2 Kings 18:12)
7. False (2 Cor. 7:13–14)
8. False (James 3:3)
9. True (1 Kings 17:2–3)
10. False (Gen. 3:11–13)
11. True (Jon. 1:1–17)
12. True (1 Pet. 3:19–20)
13. False (2 Thess. 1:8–9)
14. True (Heb. 13:17)
15. False (Exod. 12:24–28)
16. False (Num. 32:11–12)
17. True (Rom. 15:15–18)

Have a Nice Trip!
Pages 257-258

1. Egypt (Matt. 2:13)
2. Abram (Abraham) (Gen. 12:1–4)
3. Timothy (1 Thess. 2:17–3:2)
4. Jericho (Luke 10:30)
5. Jonah (Jon. 1:1–3)
6. Nehemiah (Neh. 1:1–3; 2:1–6)
7. Babylon (Dan. 1:1–2)
8. Philippi (Acts 20:6)
9. James (James 4:13–15)
10. Joseph (Gen. 37:23–28)
11. Timnah (Judg. 14:1–7)
12. Sodom (Gen. 13:11–12)
13. Naomi (Ruth 1:1–7, 19)
14. Galilee (Mark 1:14)
15. Elijah (1 Kings 19:1–4)

Lot's to Think About
Pages 259-260

   A. 13 (19:26)
   B. 2 (13:8–9)
   C. 6 (18:16–33)
   D. 8 (19:6–8)
   E. 4 (14:11–12)
   F. 12 (19:17–22)
   G. 15 (19:31–35)
   H. 10 (19:12–13)
   I. 7 (19:1)
   J. 16 (19:36–38)
   K. 1 (13:1)
   L. 14 (19:30)
   M. 3 (13:10–12)
   N. 5 (14:13–15)
   O. 9 (19:11)
   P. 11 (19:15–16)

You Can't Eat That!
Pages 262-266

   1. D. (Lev. 7:24)
   2. B. (Prov. 23:29–33)
   3. A. (Acts 21:25)
   4. D. (Lev. 7:25)
   5. B. (Gen. 41:14–21)
   6. C. (Exod. 22:31)
   7. C. (Deut. 12:23)
   8. A. (1 Cor. 8:8)
   9. D. (Lev. 7:33)
  10. B. (Lev. 10:8)
  11. C. (Deut. 14:9–10)
  12. D. (Matt. 6:25, 31)
  13. B. (Deut. 14:11–18)
  14. A. (Gen. 2:17)
  15. A. (Luke 6:1–5)
  16. C. (Deut. 14:4–7)

17. B. (Matt. 4:1–4)
18. D. (Deut. 14:19)

"Sorry About That, Chief!"
Pages 267-269

1. True (Jon. 1:12)
2. True (Gen. 33:3)
3. True (Matt. 14:6–11)
4. False (Gen. 6:8) (it was Noah!)
5. True (Rom. 9:2–4)
6. True (Luke 22:45)
7. False (1 Sam. 24:1–22)
8. False (Eccles. 7:3)
9. False (Rev. 21:1–4, 22:1)
10. True (Gen. 3:16)
11. True (Ps. 51) (see heading)
12. False (It was Jeremiah)
13. True (Matt. 27:3–5)
14. True (1 Chron. 19:1–5)
15. True (Job 2:11–12)
16. False (Dan. 3:28–30)

I See . . . Dead People!
Pages 270-272

1. Matthew (Matt. 27:50–53)
2. Cain (Gen. 4:10)
3. Jairus (Mark 5:22–24, 35–43)
4. Moses (Jude 9)
5. Eutychus (Acts 20:7–12)
6. Ephron (Gen. 23:1–20)
7. Sodom, Egypt (Rev. 11:7–8)
8. Jezebel (2 Kings 9:30–35)
9. Joseph of Arimathea (Matt. 27:58)
10. Joseph (Gen. 50:1–2)
11. Ishmael son of Nethania (Jer. 41:7)
12. Ezekiel (Ezek. 37:1–14)
13. Prayer (and fasting) (Mark 9:14–29)
14. Jeremiah (Jer. 16:1–4)

15. Zechariah son of Jehoiada (2 Chron. 24:20–22)
16. Samuel (1 Sam. 28:7–19)

"Olden Goldies"
Pages 274-275

1. E. (Dan. 2:32)
2. D. (Gen. 2:11)
3. G. (1 Pet. 1:7)
4. L. (Prov. 25:1)
5. H. (Matt. 2:11)
6. J. (Exod. 39:1–2)
7. A. (Exod. 35:30–36:1)
8. K. (1 Kings 10:1–10)
9. B. (Jer. 51:7)
10. F. (Job 23:10)
11. C. (2 Tim. 2:20–21)
12. I.

EASING UP—WINDING DOWN

You've been hitting it pretty hard, and regardless of what our Bible celebrities might say or think, **I'm** still proud of you! But we're not home free just yet. Let's stay psyched as we taper off just a bit. We'll start with something I like to call:

"DO YOU KNOW WHERE IT'S AT?"

(If the title sounds a bit 60-ish, there's a good reason for it!)

In this fill-in-the-blank exercise, simply select the book of the Bible from which the story is taken, and write it in the corresponding blank. To make it even easier, I'm giving you a list. If you want to show me how infinite your knowledge is, cover the list with a sheet of paper, your hand, or the Wal-Mart flier lying on the table, and then try it **without** using the list!

Esther	1 Chronicles	Revelation
2 Kings	Luke	Zechariah
Philemon	Ezra	Mark
Psalms	1 Samuel	1 Thessalonians
Ecclesiastes	Acts	Joel
Genesis	Matthew	1 John

_____ 1. An angel kills 185,000 Assyrians

_____ 2. Deals with a slave named Onesimus

_____ 3. A devastating locust attack

_____ 4. The day of the Lord will come as unexpectedly as "a thief in the night"

_____ 5. Life "under the sun" is meaningless

_____ 6. The death of Joseph son of Jacob

_____ 7. Begins with a prophecy from Isaiah about John the Baptist

_____ 8. Saul commits suicide

_____ 9. A vision of locusts that looked like horses with human faces, women's hair, lions' teeth, and golden crowns

_____ 10. The thief on the cross seeks mercy from Jesus

_____ 11. A vision of a man standing among myrtle trees

_____ 12. Paul and Barnabas split up after a heated argument

_____ 13. Herod puts out a decree to kill all boys in Bethlehem ages two and under

_____ 14. This New Testament book refers to the slaying of Abel by Cain

_____ 15. After his adulterous affair with Bathsheba, David cries out, "Have mercy on me, O God"

_____ 16. The prophets Haggai and Zechariah show up to encourage the people to rebuild the temple in Jerusalem

_____ 17. A wicked man is hung on a 75-foot-tall gallows

_____ 18. Eli the priest accused Elkanah's first wife, Hannah, of being drunk (she was praying at the time!)

Now let me tell you where the *answers is at*–page 314. (Did I mention that I'm an *english* major?)

It's time for another sequel. Unlike Hollywood, I'm not going to beat you to death with "Rocky 37" or "Star Wars 14: Darth Vader Challenges Jarjar Binks to an Ewok-Throwing Contest." Nope, not me. I'm only featuring the high quality stuff.

IT'S ALL RELATIVE (PART TWO)

There was so much interesting stuff left in this category, I just couldn't help myself. True or false?

___ 1. The beheading of John the Baptist indirectly involved King Herod's brother, Philip.

___ 2. At its peak, Solomon's harem contained 450 queens and wives, and 150 concubines.

___ 3. Since Sarah (Sarai) was unable to have children, she told her husband Abraham (Abram) to father a child with her maidservant, whose name was Rebekah.

___ 4. The Bible briefly mentions a battle with the Philistines in which one of Goliath's brothers was killed.

___ 5. Although Daniel is generally believed to be the author of the book that bears his name, almost no information is offered concerning his family.

___ 6. According to Matthew, the first four disciples Jesus called were two sets of brothers.

___ 7. Satan's first assault on Job's family included the death of his three sons and seven daughters.

___ 8. The father of Samuel had two wives.

___ 9. On the road to Gaza, Philip converted an Ethiopian eunuch, then baptized the man and his wife and four children.

___ 10. King David's sons were royal advisers and chief officials at his side.

___11. In the incident recorded in 1 Corinthians 5, regarding incest in the church, the case involved a man and his daughter-in-law.

___12. Jesus had a grandfather named Jacob.

___13. Paul writes to Timothy that widows with families should be financially assisted by the church since those same families help others.

___14. Zibiah was the mother of Joash, who became king at the age of seven.

___15. According to Genesis, Noah's son Ham was the father of Nimrod, the great warrior.

___16. When the men of the tribe of Benjamin needed wives, they kidnapped women from Shiloh and married them.

___17. At the close of 1 Peter, Peter refers to Mark as his "son."

___18. David was King Saul's son-in-law for a time.

___19. When the sealed book described in Revelation 5 is opened, the first figures to appear are three angelic sisters.

___20. Paul mentions to Philemon that when he comes to visit the believers in Colosse, he will stay with his mother's brother.

Enough relatives for you? Me too! See if you relate to the answers on page 314.

How about a break? Here's my list of the

TOP TEN PROBLEMS
ASSOCIATED WITH NOAH'S ARK

10. Giraffes necking
 9. Ark cited by Water Patrol for expired registration
 8. Midnight buffets got out of control
 7. Whenever Noah let animals vote, majority always carried by rabbits
 6. Animals complained about seafood, but grew strangely quiet when asked to provide other options
 5. Limited ports of call
 4. Not enough life jackets
 3. Faulty compass foiled plans to settle in Hawaii
 2. Large animals intentionally rocking the boat just for laughs
 1. Everyone wanted the seat by the window

Okay, break's over! Back to the workout!

ANOTHER TYPICAL DAY ON NOAH'S ARK.

IT'S A NUMBERS GAME

The Bible contains a lot of numbers; in fact, it even has a book by that name! But the following questions come from **through-out** the Bible, and I have a feeling some of these might surprise you. Perhaps a **number** of them will.

1. How many trained men did Abraham take with him, when he went to rescue his nephew, Lot, from the four kings who had captured him?

   A. 5,000
   B. 318
   C. 70
   D. None; he went alone

2. According to the parable of the wicked servant, what was the debt that the servant owed his master?

   A. 100 denarii
   B. 40 pieces of silver
   C. his firstborn child
   D. 10,000 talents
   E. 18 holes of golf at Potiphar Pines

3. How many men were on board the ship when it struck a sand bar and broke apart, forcing Paul and everyone else to swim in to the beach on Malta?

   A. 44
   B. 276
   C. 100
   D. 7
   E. 24, including Noah, Captain Steubing, George Clooney, Ernest Borgnine, and John Paul Jones

4. How large was David's army when he settled in the Philistine town of Ziklag?

    A. He had no army; he traveled with twelve friends
    B. 7,000 men
    C. 600 men
    D. 2,400 men
    E. Army? David was a Marine!

5. According to Ezekiel, a special portion of land was to be given to the Zadokites (as a reward for their faithfulness), and in its center was to be a sanctuary for the Lord. What were the dimensions of that parcel?

    A. 500 paces long by 250 paces wide
    B. 3,000 paces long by 3,000 paces wide
    C. 4,000 cubits long by 1,000 cubits wide
    D. 25,000 cubits long by 10,000 cubits wide
    E. Unknown, as the deed was never recorded at the courthouse

6. According to Paul's lengthy list in 2 Corinthians, which is accurate?

    A. He was stoned three times; flogged once; shipwrecked twice; and given 39 lashes on four occasions
    B. He was stoned twice; given 39 lashes six times; twice beaten with rods; shipwrecked three times
    C. He was given 39 lashes five different times; beaten with rods three times; stoned once; and shipwrecked three times
    D. He was beaten with rods once; stoned twice; given 40 lashes many times; and shipwrecked once
    E. He was given "time outs" five different times; sent to bed twice without dessert; and was once grounded for a week

7. Paul instructed Timothy that a widow must be at least this age before she could be put on the list for church assistance:

   A. 60
   B. 55
   C. 75
   D. 70

8. Zephaniah talks of a remnant of humble people being left in Israel, who were spared from God's wrath. How many are included?

   A. 144,000
   B. 5,000 godly men, with their families
   C. 12,000 men of Judah
   D. No number is given

9. How many pillars support the "house of wisdom" mentioned in Proverbs 9?

   A. Seven
   B. Four
   C. Twelve
   D. "A multitude"

10. How much barley did Boaz pour into Ruth's shawl?

    A. Two ephahs
    B. Six measures
    C. Three small baskets
    D. Two omers
    E. Just barley enough to keep her alive

11. When Abraham "negotiated" with God regarding the number of righteous men in Sodom, with what number did Abraham start and with what number did he end his plea?

    A. 100/12
    B. 50/10

C. 70/5

D. 40/2

12. How many sheep did Job have after his travails?

A. None

B. 2,000

C. 6,000

D. 14,000

E. Unknown, as counting them was shear madness

13. How long did Nehemiah and his brothers refuse the food that was rightfully allotted to the governor?

A. Seven months

B. Five years

C. Twelve years

D. Nehemiah refused it throughout his stay, but those who served as his assistants accepted it

14. According to Mark's account, how many loaves and fish did Jesus use to feed five thousand men?

A. Five loaves and two fish

B. Two loaves and five fish

C. Five loaves and seven fish

D. Seven loaves and five fish

E. Two loaves of Aunt Millie's Cracked Wheat Bread and a bucketful of carp

15. According to Revelation 4, how many thrones surrounded the throne in heaven?

A. 24

B. 7

C. 144

D. 70

E. The throne is surrounded by angels, not thrones

16. How old was Jesus when his parents unintentionally left him behind following the Passover Feast in Jerusalem?

    A. About ten years old
    B. Eight years old
    C. Fifteen years old
    D. Twelve years old
    E. Roughly sixty

17. How many provinces received Mordecai's orders allowing the Jews to fight against potential attackers? (If you know this, I'm like . . . flabbergasted!)

    A. 17
    B. 39
    C. 127
    D. 234
    E. Only the ones who had email

18. On what day of the month were the Israelites to slaughter and eat the lambs for the celebration of Passover?

    A. The first day of the month
    B. They were to select them on the tenth, then slaughter and eat them on the fourteenth
    C. The were to select them on the seventh day, slaughter them and place the blood over the doorpost; the meat could not be eaten until the next day
    D. All of the above took place on the seventh day
    E. The day changed each year according to the Jewish calendar

Now, to discover how big of a number you just did on yourself, turn to the answers on page 315!

HIGH FIVES FOR METAPHORS

The Bible is rife with colorful comparisons, those elements of language we refer to as metaphors and similes. See if you can match the items in the following list with their biblical "descriptions":

___1. A rock

___2. A fleeting vapor

___3. The gate of heaven

___4. A thief in the night

___5. Springs without water

___6. Doves

___7. An ornament to grace your neck

___8. A fire

___9. A dog

___10. Scales

___11. Straw before the wind

___12. Turbulent as the waters

___13. Sheep

A. The tongue

B. A bride's eyes

C. Goliath

D. Sound judgment

E. Bethel

F. The day of the Lord

G. The people of Israel

H. Coating on Paul's eyes

I. Samson's wife

J. Peter

K. The wicked

L. Evil men

M. David & his men

N. One speaking eloquently without love

O. A fortune made by lying

___14. As fierce as a wild
 bear

___15. A heifer

___16. A resounding gong

___17. Drawn swords

P. Reuben

Q. The words of a man
 with "war in his
 heart"

Now, let's make another comparison . . . **your** answers to the correct ones on page 315!

I'm tellin' ya, this next part could get a little dangerous. So just remember . . .

YOU'VE BEEN WARNED!

True/False

____ 1. Paul mentioned that no matter what city he visited, the Holy Spirit continued to warn him about prison and potential hardships to come.

____ 2. When Lot warned his prospective sons in-law that God was about to destroy Sodom, they immediately gathered their belongings and headed to the mountains.

____ 3. King Nebuchadnezzar told Shadrach, Meshach, and Abednego that unless they worshiped the golden image he had created, they would be thrown into boiling oil.

____ 4. According to Matthew's account, the wise men were warned in a dream not to return to Herod. In the very next verse, Joseph receives a second warning in a dream.

____ 5. When Jonah warned the citizens of Nineveh of God's approaching judgment, they immediately believed and repented.

____ 6. When Jesus discussed the "second coming," he referred to Sarah's scoffing as an example of human disbelief.

____ 7. Although God made Ezekiel a "watchman" over Israel, he was not required by God to exhort the wicked to conform to God's laws.

___8. According to Revelation 8, a warning to earth is given by an eagle before the trumpet blasts of three angels.

___9. When Jeremiah confronted Judah's people at the courtyard of the temple and warned them of the desolation to come, they wanted to kill him.

___10. "You will deny me three times," Jesus told Peter. "Upon the third denial, a rooster will attack you and try to peck you to death."

___11. Moses warned Pharaoh before some of the plagues, but not before all of them.

___12. Paul cautioned Timothy about allowing a new convert or a man with a bad reputation to become an overseer in the church.

___13. Moses exhorted his people not to add to or subtract from God's law, and used the fates of the people who worshiped the Baal of Peor as an example of judgment.

___14. Paul instructed Titus that a divisive person should be given two warnings, then tried before the whole congregation before he is removed from the body of believers.

___15. Just before Joshua died, he admonished the people to remember to keep the Passover and other holy feasts.

___16. Prior to King Jehoram's death, he received a letter from Elijah the prophet, warning Jehoram that he would contract a terrible lingering disease of the bowels. (Now you must ask yourself, would I make this up?)

_____17. One of the last things found in the book of Revelation is a strong warning against adding to or subtracting from the author's words.

Warning: Some of your answers may not be the same as those listed on page 316. In that case, you will be wrong. However, unlike smoking, being wrong is not necessarily hazardous to your health—depending, of course, on what you're wrong **about!**

("No, honey, I'm sure the Titanic will get us home safely.")

I DON'T THINK SO!

Few people can name all sixty-six books of the Bible, but many will recognize most of them. The following list contains twelve impostors. See if you can spot them.

Nehemiah	Acts	3 Timothy	Colossians
Ruth	2 Kings	Haggai	Silas
Nahum	3 John	Job	Letters
Numbers	Jude	Zechariah	Gideon
Ezra	James	Zephaniah	Hezekiah
Ephesians	John	Abraham	2 Corinthians
Hebrews	Micah	Luke	Philemon
Elijah	Galatians	2 Peter	Judges
Nebuchadnezzar	Romans	Psalms	2 Philippians
Esther	Song of Songs	Joel	Amos
Joshua	Revelation	Sidonians	Ecclesiastes
Leviticus	1 Kings	Jonah	Noah
Lamentations	Ezekiel	Jacob	Exodus
Proverbs	Obadiah		

Ready for the list of "Wannebes"? They're on page 316.
You're still working pretty hard. Let's take a quick humor

break! Before I give you this Top Ten list, let me refresh your memory about the story.

Nebuchadnezzar's descendant Belshazzar was partying with his nobles, and they were offering praise to the gods of gold and silver, of which their goblets were made. Suddenly, a hand appeared and began writing on the wall:

MENE, MENE, TEKEL, PARSIN

Of course, the king nearly collapsed from fear, but once he'd composed himself, he called upon his astrologers and diviners to interpret the writing, offering great rewards to the successful candidate.

They failed, and Daniel subsequently solved the mystery. Here then are the

TOP TEN INTERPRETATIONS OF THE HANDWRITING ON THE WALL OFFERED BY BELSHAZZAR'S SOOTHSAYERS

10. "Eenie, meenie, minie, moe"
9. "The British are coming, the British are coming!"
8. "What you see is what you get"
7. "Take two aspirin and call me in the morning"
6. "We're looking for a few good men"
5. "Here's lookin' at you, kid"
4. "Where's the beef?"
3. "Is that your final answer?"
2. "Yes, Belshazzar, there is a Santa Claus"
1. "Eat at Joe's"

SAYS WHO?
(PART TWO: NEW TESTAMENT)

Identify the speaker in the following quotes. Why? Because I sez so!

1. "Sirs, what must I do to be saved?"

   A. A centurion
   B. An Ethiopian eunuch
   C. Ananias
   D. A jailer at Philippi

2. "You are Israel's teacher . . ."

   A. Nicodemus, talking to Jesus
   B. Jesus, addressing Nicodemus
   C. Peter, to Gamaliel
   D. Paul, to Agrippa

3. " . . . he will clear his threshing floor, gathering his wheat into the barn and burning up the chaff with unquenchable fire."

   A. The apostle John
   B. Jesus
   C. John the Baptist
   D. Paul
   E. Simon the Amish

4. "I do not permit a woman to teach or to have authority over a man; she must be silent."

   A. Paul
   B. Peter
   C. Jesus
   D. Timothy

5. "Is it lawful for a man to divorce his wife for any and every reason?"

   A. Some Pharisees
   B. Judas Iscariot
   C. A certain scribe
   D. The Sadducees
   E. Mickey Rooney

6. "These men are not drunk, as you suppose. It's only nine in the morning!"

   A. Stephen
   B. Saul (before becoming "Paul")
   C. Peter
   D. Luke
   E. Moe, the bartender

7. "Fear God and give him glory, because the hour of his judgment has come. Worship him who made the heavens, the earth, the sea and the springs of water."

   A. The writer of Hebrews (author unknown)
   B. An angel flying in midair
   C. Jude
   D. James
   E. Demetrius the silversmith

8. "We have found this man to be a troublemaker, stirring up riots among the Jews all over the world."

   A. Caiaphas, the high priest
   B. Pilate
   C. Felix, the governor
   D. Tertullus, a lawyer

9. "Jesus, Son of David, have mercy on me!"

   A. A demon that had come out of a child
   B. Peter's mother-in-law

C. A leper lowered from a roof
D. A blind man named Bartimaeus
E. Lola, the first Unitarian

10. "The Lord has done this for me. In these days he has shown his favor and taken away my disgrace among the people."

A. Mary
B. Paul
C. Elizabeth
D. Matthew

11. "Do you understand what you are reading?"

A. Peter
B. Philip
C. Jesus
D. Ananias
E. Anyone standing nearby when I open a comic book

12. "Go, pour out the seven bowls of God's wrath on the earth."

A. A loud voice from the temple
B. The seven thunders
C. The great prostitute
D. The angel clothed in scarlet
E. The devil with the blue dress on

13. "Take a guard. Go, make the tomb as secure as you know how."

A. Joseph of Arimathea
B. Pilate
C. Barabbas
D. Mary Magdalene

14. "Son, remember that in your lifetime you received your good things, while Lazarus received bad things."

   A. God
   B. Peter
   C. The prodigal son's father
   D. Abraham

15. "See, the Lord is coming with thousands upon thousands of his holy ones to judge everyone, and to convict the ungodly . . ."

   A. James, quoting Isaiah
   B. Paul, quoting Ezekiel
   C. Jude, quoting Enoch
   D. Peter, quoting Jeremiah
   E. Stone Philips, quoting Billy Graham

16. "You are out of your mind, Paul. Your great learning is driving you insane."

   A. Agrippa
   B. Caesar
   C. Festus
   D. Publius
   E. Freud

"Now," sez I, "I'm gonna tell yas how it really is." (That means the answers are comin' up on page 317!)

THERE'S SOMETHING FISHY GOING ON!

Fish have been around forever, and so have fish **stories**. Even the Good Book has its share. So without further carping, take the bait and flounder through the following ten fillet-in-the-blank questions. (Sorry.)

1. Jesus instructed Peter to throw out his line, pull in the first fish he caught, and take a _____ from its mouth.

2. Contrary to the oft-repeated error, the Bible says it was a "great fish" (not a "whale") that swallowed _____.

3. According to the Genesis account, God created fish (living creatures in the waters) on the _____ day.

4. The Old Testament writer of _____ (book?) uses the analogy of fish being caught in a net to illustrate men being trapped by unexpected peril.

5. _____ taught Peter and John to play "Go Fish!"

6. _____ and _____ were in a boat, preparing a fishing net, when Jesus called them to follow him.

7. According to John's account, the two fish and five small loaves that Jesus used to feed five thousand men were supplied by a _____.

8. Moses specifically mentions the image of fish as something that should not be replicated for use as _____.

9. After _____ was humbled by having a hook put in his nose, and carted off to Babylon by the king of Assyria, he cried out to God, and God brought him back to Jerusalem. There, he rebuilt the outer wall of Jerusalem west of Gihon as far as the entrance of the Fish Gate.

10. The creatures living in the water that were acceptable for consumption had to have _____ and _____.

The answers are flopping around on page 317, but if you miss some, please don't get crabby.

THE HOKEY POKEY

Lots of Bible personalities did time, for a variety of reasons—often because they said unpopular things around the wrong people. (Glad **I've** never done that.)

Your task is to match the incarcerated person with his (or her) crime. This should prevent you from going stir-crazy for a while.

___1. Satan

___2. Paul

___3. Samson

___4. Jeremiah

___5. Paul & Silas

___6. Joseph

___7. John the Baptist

___8. Micaiah

___9. John

___10. Hanani the seer

___11. Simeon

___12. O. J. Simpson

___13. Jehoiachin

___14. Spirits

A. He was imprisoned by a king, even though the king considered him to be a righteous man

B. He was to be housed in the pokey as security for a pledge

C. He was imprisoned in the barracks for his own protection

D. Tossed in the hooscow—he never told the king what the king wanted to hear

E. "If the glove doesn't fit, you must acquit"

F. In exile on Patmos

G. He was released from prison after a mere 1000 years

H. Rebuked King Asa—landed in jail

I. Bound in bronze shackles, his prison sentence was a "grind"

J. Incarceration took place after a severe flogging (all for talking to a slave girl)

K. After a long prison term, he was released, and ate often at the king's table

L. While a prisoner, he became an assistant to the prison warden

M. Visited by Christ while in prison

N. His confinement occurred during Babylon's siege of Jerusalem

Now, let's see if I can find the answers in this big house. Oops, maybe I'll have to go up the river to get them—nope, they're right here by my pen, on page 318.

"Samson here, just like I promised. Hey, I'm pretty impressed that I found you here, seein' as my eyes aren't what they used to be (or maybe I should say aren't **where** they used to be!). Well, you must've survived another part of the workout, and pretty soon you'll be as strong as me, well, I mean after my hair grows back and all. Wait a minute, my hair **is** growing out! Take me over to those temple pillars, okay? Thanks. Now I'm gonna give you to the count of twenty to get outta here. One . . . two . . ."

(Rumble, rumble, CRASH! "EEEEEYYYAAHHHH!")

"Hello, Timnah, this is Phyllis Steen for the Ancient News. Today Samson apparently regained his amazing strength and destroyed Dagon's temple and everyone in it, including himself. Apparently, no one thought to give Samson a regular shave and this was the result. Rescue workers say Samson may have exploited a hairline crack in the temple, and received support from his own new hairline. Film at eleven."

EASING UP—WINDING DOWN
ANSWERS

"Do You Know Where It's At?"
Pages 285-287

1. 2 Kings (19:35)
2. Philemon (10–19)
3. Joel (1:4)
4. 1 Thessalonians (5:2)
5. Ecclesiastes (1:14)
6. Genesis (50:22–26)
7. Mark (1:2–7)
8. 1 Chronicles (10:4)
9. Revelation (9:3–8)
10. Luke (23:40–43)
11. Zechariah (1:8–17)
12. Acts (15:36–40)
13. Matthew (2:16)
14. 1 John (3:12)
15. Psalms (51:1)
16. Ezra (5:1–2)
17. Esther (7:9–10)
18. 1 Samuel (1:12–18)

It's All Relative
Pages 288-289

1. True (Matt. 14:3–11)
2. False (1 Kings 11:3)
3. False (Gen. 16:1–4)
4. True (1 Chron. 20:5)
5. True (Dan. 1:3–7)
6. True (Matt. 4:18–21)
7. False (Job 1:2, 8–19)
8. True (1 Sam. 1:1–2, 19–20)
9. False (Acts 8:26) (If you missed this, I'm worried!)
10. True (2 Sam. 8:18; 1 Chron. 18:17)
11. False (1 Cor. 5:1)
12. True (Matt. 1:16)
13. False (1 Tim. 5:3–16)
14. True (2 Chron. 24:1)

15. False (Gen. 10:8)
16. True (Judg. 21:15–23)
17. True (1 Pet. 5:13)
18. True (1 Sam. 18:17–27)
19. False (Rev. 6:2)
20. False (Philem. 22)

It's a Numbers Game
Pages 291-295

1. B. (Gen. 14:14)
2. D. (Matt. 18:24)
3. B. (Acts 27:37)
4. C. (1 Sam. 27:2)
5. D. (Ezek. 48:9–11)
6. C. (2 Cor. 11:24–25)
7. A. (1 Tim. 5:9)
8. D. (Zeph 2:9; 3:13)
9. A. (Prov. 9:1)
10. B. (Ruth 3:15)
11. B. (Gen. 18 K22–33)
12. D. (Job 42:12)
13. C. (Neh. 5:14)
14. A. (Mark 6:41)
15. A. (Rev. 4:4)
16. D. (Luke 2:42)
17. C. (Esther 8:9)
18. B. (Exod. 12:3–8)

High Fives for Metaphors
Pages 296-297

1. J. (Matt. 16:18)
2. O. (Prov. 21:6)
3. E. (Gen. 28:16–19)
4. F. (1 Thess. 5:2)
5. L. (2 Pet. 2:17)
6. B. (Song of Sol. 4:1)
7. D. (Prov. 3:21–22)
8. A. (James 3:6)

9. C. (1 Sam. 17:43)
10. H. (Acts 9:18)
11. K. (Job 21:17–18)
12. P. (Gen. 49:3–4)
13. G. (1 Chron. 21:17)
14. M. (2 Sam. 17:8)
15. I. (Judg. 14:18)
16. N. (1 Cor. 13:1)
17. Q. (Ps. 55:21)

You've Been Warned!
Pages 298-300

1. True (Acts 20:23)
2. False (Gen. 19:14)
3. False (Dan. 3:15)
4. True (Matt. 2:12–13)
5. True (Jon. 3:4–10)
6. False (Luke 17:30–32)
7. False (Ezek. 3:16–19)
8. True (Rev. 8:13)
9. True (Jer. 26:2–11)
10. False (Matt. 26:34, 69–75) (Although legend has it he was henpecked at home.)
11. True (Exod. 7–12)
12. True (1 Tim. 3:6–7)
13. True (Deut. 4:1–4)
14. False (Titus 3:10)
15. False (Josh. 24:19–23)
16. True (2 Chron. 21:12–20)
17. True (Rev. 22:18–19)

I Don't Think So!
Page 301

1. Hezekiah
2. 3 Timothy (There are only two.)
3. Elijah
4. Gideon (He got an organization!)
5. Abraham

6. Nebuchadnezzar
7. 2 Philippians
8. Noah
9. Sidonians
10. Silas
11. Letters
12. Jacob

Says Who?
Pages 304-307

1. D. (Acts 16:27–31)
2. B. (John 3:10)
3. C. (Matt. 3:12)
4. A. (1 Tim. 2:12)
5. A. (Matt. 19:3)
6. C. (Acts 2:15)
7. B. (Rev. 14:6–7)
8. D. (Acts 24:1–5)
9. D. (Mark 10:46–47)
10. C. (Luke 1:25)
11. B. (Acts 8:30)
12. A. (Rev. 16:1)
13. B. (Matt. 27:65)
14. D. (Luke 16:25)
15. C. (Jude 1:14)
16. C. (Acts 26:24)

There's Something Fishy Going On
Pages 308-309

1. Coin (Matt. 17:27)
2. Jonah (Jon. 1:17)
3. Fifth Day (Gen. 1:20–23)
4. Ecclesiastes (Eccles. 9:12)
5. Nobody! (You'll just have to trust me on this one.)
6. James, John (Matt. 4:21–22)
7. Boy (John 6:9)
8. Idols (Deut. 4:15–18)
9. Manasseh (2 Chron. 33:10–14)
10. Fins, scales (Lev. 11:9)

Hokey Pokey
Pages 310-311

1. G. (Rev. 20:7)
2. C. (Acts 23:10)
3. I. (Judg. 16:21)
4. N. (Jer. 32:2)
5. J. (Acts 16:19–24)
6. L. (Gen. 39:20–23)
7. A. (Mark 6:17–20)
8. D. (2 Chron. 18:7, 25–26)
9. F. (Rev. 1:9)
10. H. (2 Chron. 16:7–10)
11. B. (Gen. 42:18–24)
12. E. (Johnnie Cochran)
13. K. (2 Kings 25:27–30)
14. M. (1 Pet. 3:18–19)

HITTING THE SHOWERS

Yes, it's that time when we get to rid ourselves of one kind of water on our bodies by standing naked under another kind of water. Seems kind of silly doesn't it? Anyway, since we're on the subject, let's see how many of the following unclad people you can identify.

HEY—NO PEEKING!

1. When the prophet Ezekiel said, "you . . . exposed your nakedness in your promiscuity with your lovers," he was referring to

   A. Judah
   B. Gomer (the wife of Hosea)
   C. Potiphar's wife
   D. Jerusalem
   E. Madonna

2. Hosea claims that God will strike Israel and strip her as naked as

   A. The day she was born
   B. A desert
   C. Adam's wife Eve on the day she was created
   D. A shaved lamb
   E. Both A & B
   F. None of the above

3. According to Matthew's account, what happened to Jesus' clothes after his crucifixion?

   A. The chief priests took them
   B. The soldiers cast lots for them
   C. Jesus' mother and Mary Magdalene took the clothes
   D. Joseph of Arimathea purchased them

4. What happened just prior to Ham seeing his father's nakedness?

   A. Noah became drunk on wine
   B. Noah had bathed in the Euphrates River
   C. Noah was washing his garment
   D. Noah's wife was mending his garment
   E. Noah had been working on his tan

5. According to Amos, when the Lord judges Israel, "_____ will flee naked on that day."

   A. All the idolaters who have disobeyed the Lord
   B. Mothers and children
   C. The sons of Jacob
   D. The bravest warriors

6. Luke tells of a demon-possessed man who didn't wear clothes. Prior to being healed by Jesus, where had this man lived?

   A. Beneath the synagogue
   B. With Peter's brother-in-law
   C. In the tombs
   D. In the wilderness
   E. At the "Sun Demon's Nudist Resort"

7. "Go down, sit in the dust. . . . Your nakedness will be exposed and your shame uncovered." This is part of the Lord's judgment of

   A. Persia
   B. Babylon
   C. Israel
   D. Assyria
   E. None of the above

8. After eating the forbidden fruit, Adam and Eve quickly realized they were naked. Who was the first to mention it?

    A. The serpent
    B. Adam
    C. Eve
    D. God
    E. Eve's mother

9. Jesus said, "Behold, I come like a thief!" What two actions did he recommend to avoid going naked?

    A. Be continually in the Spirit
    B. Stay awake
    C. Worship the Lamb
    D. Refuse the seal (mark) of the beast
    E. Keep your clothes with you

10. When Paul asked rhetorically if nakedness could separate a believer from Jesus Christ, he also mentioned all of the following except

    A. Famine
    B. Trouble
    C. Danger
    D. Imprisonment
    E. Persecution

11. This minor prophet condemned the person who would get his neighbors drunk "so that he can gaze on their naked bodies." (Yep, that's what it says!)

    A. Habakkuk
    B. Zephaniah
    C. Joel
    D. Micah

12. Following the giving of the Ten Commandments, a rule about exposing oneself is mentioned. It concerns

   A. Approaching the holy mountain unclothed
   B. Staying covered while in the Tent of Meeting
   C. Exposing oneself while climbing steps to the altar of the Lord
   D. Mooning the enemy tribes

13. She remained childless, ostensibly for rebuking her husband about dressing immodestly while dancing.

   A. Naomi
   B. Jezebel
   C. Vashti
   D. Michal
   E. Chloe

14. This prophet spent three years "in the buff" in order to be a sign against Egypt and Cush.

   A. Isaiah
   B. Jeremiah
   C. Habakkuk
   D. Daniel
   E. Elisha

   Now, I will disrobe the answers, and we will examine the nekked truth! (I'm going to double-check the answers on page 366 just to cover my tail!)

I've always been a big Moses fan. You have to admit, his story is unique. From his beginnings in a floating crib, to the Egypt/Pharaoh thing, to his mountaintop experiences—well, it just makes sense to keep the legend alive with . . .

WAY TO GO, MO! (PART THREE)

(The Last of the "Mo" Hicans)

True/False

___ 1. The book of Numbers mentions a man named Hobab, whom Moses entreated to accompany and guide the people through the desert. Hobab was Moses' brother-in-law.

___ 2. When the people began complaining about not having meat to eat, Moses told God, "If this is how you're going to treat me, put me to death."

___ 3. The Lord sent thousands of quail to feed the Israelites, and when he saw how they immediately praised him for it, God was sorry that he had been angry at them.

___ 4. Aaron and Miriam began to speak against Moses because he remained unmarried while encouraging the people to marry.

___ 5. As a result of their transgressions, God struck both Aaron and Miriam with leprosy.

___ 6. Of the twelve men Moses sent to scout Canaan, only Joshua encouraged the people to go and take the land immediately.

___ 7. After the people threatened mutiny against Moses and go back to Egypt, God wanted to kill them, but Moses pleaded for their lives.

___8. All of the men responsible for the bad reports of Canaan died of a plague.

___9. The next day after Korah and his followers were swallowed by the earth for their rebellion, the Israelites repented.

___10. When Moses placed twelve staffs (one for each of the tribes) in the Tent of Meeting, Aaron's staff budded and produced almonds.

___11. Thin slices of the staff from the tribe of Frito Lay were so incredibly tasty that none of the Israelites could eat just one.

___12. The Lord warned Aaron that he and his family would bear the responsibility for any offenses against the sanctuary, and expressly told him that anyone who came near the sanctuary was to be put to death.

___13. Miriam died at the Desert of Zin, just prior to Moses striking the rock that produced water.

___14. Although Moses made two reasonable offers to the king of Edom, requesting passage through his country, the king refused to allow it.

___15. After being bitten by one of the venomous snakes sent by the Lord, Aaron died shortly before Moses made the bronze serpent.

___16. Balaam was initially contacted to assist Israel regarding a land dispute with the Moabites.

___17. Moses told the people that once they entered Canaan, they should make treaties only with tribes that could not be soundly defeated.

___18. Moses made provisions for the people to choose a king once they had settled in the promised land.

___19. Moses instructed the armies to offer distant cities the opportunity to peacefully subject themselves to the Israelites. If the people refused, the Israelites were to lay siege to that city.

___20. God gave Moses the words to a song and told him to teach it to the people.

___21. After Moses died on Mt. Nebo, Joshua and the priests buried him facing the promised land.

___22. Deuteronomy concludes by saying that "no prophet has ever shown the mighty power or performed the awesome deeds that Moses did."

And so ends the story . . . now let's "mo"—tate to the answers on page 366!

ORDER IN THE COURT!

There were enough kings in the Old Testament to keep the **average** person (I'm still fighting to work my way up to that!) confused. Do your best to arrange the following list of kings in the order the Bible states they became king—from the earliest to the latest.

To make it just a teeny bit easier, I'm dividing them into three sections which hopefully will be self-explanatory. Remember—no crowning around!

GROUP ONE: BEFORE THE DIVISION OF THE KINGDOM

Solomon	Saul	Rehoboam
David	Ish-Bosheth	Adonijah*

*Technically correct, although arguable. Just put him in the proper place!

1._____   4._____

2._____   5._____

3._____   6._____

GROUP TWO: KINGS OF JUDAH (SOUTHERN KINGDOM)

Jehoram (aka Joram)

Azariah (aka Uzziah)

Joash (aka Jehoash)

Abijah (aka Abia or Abijam)

Athaliah (a woman—Judah's
only queen)

Jehoahaz (aka Joahaz)

Jotham

Hezekiah

Asa

Jehoiakim

Jehoshaphats

Jehoiachin

Josiah (aka Josias)

Zedekiah

Rehoboam

Ahaz

Amaziah

Manasseh

Ahaziah

Amon

1._____

2._____

3._____

4._____

5._____

6._____

7._____

8._____

9._____

10._____

11._____

12._____

13._____

14._____

15._____

16._____

17._____

18._____

19._____

20._____

(Yes, I know it's difficult, but not everything in life is a walk in the park. Suck it up!)

GROUP THREE: KINGS OF ISRAEL (NORTHERN KINGDOM)

Jehoahaz
   (aka Joahaz, but not the
   same person on previous list)
Jehoash
   (again, not the same
   as previous list)
Joram
   (aka Jehoram, but I'm
   beginning to sound like
   a broken record . . . oops-
   a faulty CD!

Elah
Zechariah
Nadab
Jeroboam I
Shallum
Tibni
Zimri
Baasha
Ahaziah
   (also had a
   namesake)

Ahab
Jeroboam II
Pekah
Omri
Menahem
Pekahiah
Jehoahaz
Jehu
Hoshea

1._____

2._____

3._____

4._____

5._____

6._____

7._____

8._____

9._____

10._____

11._____

12._____

13._____

14._____

15._____

16._____

17._____

18._____

19._____

20._____

Okay, I promise we'll get to something easier (and hopefully more entertaining) right after you check your answers. But you never know when someone is going to ask you, " Hey, _____ (insert your name here), was it Menahem or Hoshea that overthrew Pekah just before Israel fell to the Assyrians?" And believe me, you'd better know the answer! So head to page 366, and congratulations if you had even a hand-ful of these in the proper order! Now, breathe a long sigh of relief and let's get out of here!

HE SAYS, SHE SAYS

The Good Book has plenty of conversations between women and men, and some examples of a woman's response to God. Select the correct responses to the following.

1. King Xerxes said to Esther, "What is it, Queen Esther? What is your request? Even up to half the kingdom, it will be given you."
   She said:

   A. "May the great king allow my uncle, Mordecai, to live in the palace."
   B. "Let the king, together with Haman, come today to a banquet I have prepared."
   C. "Allow me to return to Jerusalem, to help rebuild the city."
   D. "May the king see fit to give my people a city in the southern part of your kingdom."
   E. "I'm dying for some Tommy jeans."

2. When a Canaanite woman came to Jesus about healing her demon-possessed daughter, Jesus said, "I was sent only to the lost sheep of Israel. It is not right to take the children's bread and toss it to their dogs."
   She said:

   A. "Master, my daughter is but an innocent child."
   B. "Without God's mercy, are we not all less than dogs?"
   C. "Man does not live by bread alone, but by every word of God."
   D. "Yes, Lord, but even the dogs eat the crumbs that fall from their master's table."
   E. "Fine. If you happen to see a collie carrying a pitchfork, that'll be her."

3. The angel of the Lord discovered Hagar in the desert by a spring. He said, "Hagar, servant of Sarai, . . . where are you going?"
She said:

    A. "I'm returning to Egypt, to my own people."
    B. "To the village of Shur, to hide my shame."
    C. "I'm running away from my mistress Sarai."
    D. "I'm going into the wilderness to die."

4. Peter asked Sapphira, "Is this the price you and Ananias got for the land?"
She said:

    A. "My husband would not lie to you."
    B. "Yes, that is the price."
    C. "Would Ananias and I test the spirit of God?"
    D. "No, my husband kept back part of the money."
    E. "Yes, after you deduct the Realtor's commission and closing costs."

5. Job's wife said, "Are you still holding on to your integrity? Curse God and die!"
He said:

    A. "How shall a man curse God? Can an ox destroy his master?"
    B. "The Lord is testing me. Shall I summon my last breath before I have endured hardship?"
    C. "You are talking like a foolish woman. Shall we accept good from God, and not trouble?"
    D. "Life and death are the tools of God. He will give me rest by His own doing."
    E. "Alice, I'm gonna send you to the moon!"

6. David's servants said to Abigail, "David has sent us to you to take you to become his wife."
   She said:

   A. "Here is your maidservant, ready to serve you and wash the feet of my master's servants."
   B. "I cannot go until I have completed the customary mourning for my husband, Nabal. May my lord be merciful."
   C. "Allow your maidservant to prepare a banquet in my lord's honor."
   D. "Would such a man as David desire the widow of a Calebite?"
   E. "Sorry, I never marry before a first date."

7. King Herod said to Herodias's daughter, "Ask me for anything you want, and I'll give it to you."
   She said:

   A. "I want you to free Barabbas."
   B. "I want you to kill all male children under the age of two."
   C. "I want you to give me right now the head of John the Baptist on a platter."
   D. "I want you to make me your queen."

8. Ruth said, as she lay at the feet of Boaz, "I am your servant Ruth. Spread the corner of your garment over me, since you are a kinsman-redeemer."
   He said:

   A. "Go back to your mother-in-law, Naomi, for I am a man far too advanced in years to be your husband."
   B. "Why do you disturb my sleep? Do you not know how tiring my labor is, and that I have but a few hours to rest?"
   C. "Lie here beside me, and keep me warm. You are a noble woman, my daughter."

D. "The Lord bless you, my daughter. This kindness is greater than that which you showed earlier. . . . I will do for you all that you ask."

E. "You think you can just come in here, lie down, and start hogging the blankets? I don't think so!"

9. Martha came to Jesus and asked, "Lord, don't you care that my sister has left me to do the work by myself? Tell her to help me!"
He said:

A. "You are worried and upset about many things, but only one thing is needed. Mary has chosen what is better."

B. "Truly whoever works to serve the Son shall be blessed a hundred-fold by the Father."

C. "Both of you have shown your love for me, and I shall not judge between you. Now show the same love for one another."

D. "Woman, who made me a judge over your sister? There is only one true judge, and that is God."

E. "I think somebody needs a nap."

10. When the witch of Endor saw Samuel's spirit, she cried out at the top of her voice and said to Saul, "Why have you deceived me? You are Saul!"
He said:

A. "You will tell no one, for on that day you shall surely lose your life."

B. "Don't be afraid. What do you see?"

C. "I am your king, and my kingdom is at stake! You will do exactly as I say!"

D. "I am desperate, and Samuel is the only one who can help me. Tell me what his spirit says to you."

11. The Lord God said to Eve, "What is this you have done?"
She said:

   A. "I was very hungry, and the fruit was within reach."
   B. "The serpent deceived me, and I ate."
   C. "Adam said you would surely forgive us."
   D. "I have only eaten what you have placed here."
   E. "Did you just put us here to hassle us?"

12. Deborah sent for Barak and said to him, "Go, take with you ten thousand men of Naphtali and Zebulun and lead the way to Mount Tabor. I will lure Sisera, the commander of Jabin's army, with his chariots and his troops, to the Kishon River and give him into your hands."
He said:

   A. "If you go with me, I will go; but if you don't go with me, I won't go."
   B. "Sisera is a seasoned commander—he will not be deceived by trickery."
   C. "Our army is too small. Jabin's men will slaughter us."
   D. "It is not God's will for a woman to lead an army. I charge you to send Lappidoth, your husband, in your stead."

13. Jesus said to the Samaritan woman, "You are right when you say you have no husband. The fact is, you have had five husbands, and the man you now have is not your husband. What you have just said is quite true."
She said:

   A. "Will a Samaritan be judged as a Jew?"
   B. "You know this because you are the Messiah; forgive me, O Son of God!"
   C. "Why do you speak to me at all? Are not we Samaritans considered as dogs in your eyes?"

D. "Sir, I can see that you are a prophet."

E. "Yep, just a few more husbands and I'll be up with Liz Taylor!"

14. In Song of Songs 2, the Beloved says, "I am a rose of Sharon, a lily of the valleys."
The Lover says:

A. "A flower more fragrant does not grow upon the earth."

B. "O my love is like a red, red rose."

C. "Like a lily among thorns is my darling among the maidens."

D. "All the flowers of the verdant valleys are the marriage bed of my beloved."

15. Michal daughter of Saul and wife of David said to David, "How the king of Israel has distinguished himself today, disrobing in the sight of the slave girls of his servants as any vulgar fellow would!"
He said:

A. "How is it that you judge me, daughter of Saul? Must I remind you how the Lord dealt with the sins of your own father?"

B. "God has restored the ark of the covenant to its rightful place, and no celebration of God's mercy and righteousness is vulgar."

C. "Are you jealous of what the Lord has done? The servant girls celebrated with me—why can you not be as just?"

D. "It was before the Lord, who chose me rather than your father or anyone from his house when he appointed me ruler."

E. "It's the Hebrew Mash—and I can really shake my bootie!"

I said: the answers are on page 368.
You said: Thanks for nothing!

Time for another humor break! Here are the

TOP TEN THINGS ADAM AND EVE REALIZED AFTER THEY HAD EATEN FROM THE TREE OF KNOWLEDGE

10. The Iraqis were lying about their chemical weapons
9. Baseball salaries were way too high
8. You really needed only one credit card
7. Santa Claus wasn't real
6. The snake spoke lousy Hebrew
5. Neither of them had belly buttons
4. Professional wrestling was rigged
3. The Spice Girls had no talent at all
2. Fig leaves should be washed on "gentle" cycle
1. Not all angels were as nice as Roma Downey

See if you can name the parties who participated in these "transactions." I create the questions and you solve 'em! Okay?

IT'S A DEAL!

1. "Is not the whole land before you? If you go to the left, I'll go to the right; if you go to the right, I'll go to the left." This land deal took place between _____ and _____.

2. After a sharp disagreement, _____ selected Silas and headed for Syria, while his former companion _____ chose Mark and left for Cyprus.

3. Upon agreeing to an allotted time, King _____ gave _____ permission to return to Judah to help repair the city of his fathers.

4. Solomon's prospective kingship was in question until a "deal" was struck between _____ and _____.

5. A man filled with demons named _____ struck an agreement with _____, who allowed the demons to enter a herd of pigs.

6. _____ agreed to continue watching the flocks of _____, receiving any speckled or spotted sheep and goats, or dark-colored lambs, as payment.

7. In Revelation, the _____ offer their ruling power to the _____.

8. As part of a covenant, _____ gave _____ a robe, tunic, sword, bow, and belt.

9. _____ asked the _____ _____ what they would pay him to deliver Jesus to them, and the deal was made for thirty pieces of silver.

10. Isaiah mentions that these _____ have entered into a covenant with _____, taking refuge in a lie.

11. The speech of _____ to the _____ convinced them to release Peter and the apostles (after flogging them).

12. After hearing about Jericho and Ai, the _____ managed to trick _____ and the Israelites into a treaty.

13. _____ and _____ agreed between themselves to deceive the apostles about the profits from the sale of their land.

14. More than forty _____ conspired and took an oath not to eat until they had killed _____.

15. The writer of Hebrews mentions the first known tithing agreement, which took place when _____ gave a tenth of his war plunder to a priest named _____.

Now here's another deal: In consideration of your earnest efforts to fill in the blanks, I have placed the actual answers on page 368!

ENTER THE SANDMAN

You are getting very, verrry sleepy. When I count to three, you will become the world's best Bible trivia quiz solver! Ready? One . . . two . . . three! Now find the answers to these questions involving sleeping. Hey! Wake up!!!!

1. He taunted the prophets of Baal, asking if their god was sleeping.

   A. Elisha
   B. Ahab
   C. Balaam
   D. Elijah

2. Where were Jesus and the disciples when they fell asleep while he was praying?

   A. Mt. Nebo
   B. The upper room
   C. The Mount of Olives
   D. The porch of the temple
   E. A Yanni concert

3. While Daniel was in the lion's den, this person didn't sleep a wink.

   A. Jezebel
   B. King Darius
   C. King Nebuchadnezzar
   D. King Cyrus
   E. King Kong (He was too busy monkeying around.)

4. He was lying down, preparing to go to sleep when the Lord called to him four times.

   A. Eli
   B. Samuel
   C. Solomon
   D. Ishmael

5. Although this person was a corpse, Jesus referred to him or her as being "asleep." Then he took the person's hand, and the body returned to life.

   A. Peter's mother
   B. A man who had been killed by demons
   C. Lazarus
   D. The daughter of Jairus

6. He really hadn't had a good night's sleep in the last twenty years!

   A. Jacob
   B. Joshua
   C. Nehemiah
   D. Judah
   E. Rip Van Winkle

7. Where did Uriah sleep when David summoned him home from the war?

   A. In his own home with Bathsheba, his wife
   B. In a room in David's palace
   C. In the cave of Machpelah
   D. At the palace entrance
   E. At a bed & breakfast near the Gaza Strip

8. He had been sleeping, but he was awakened by an earthquake.

   A. Peter
   B. Paul
   C. Silas
   D. A jailer at Philippi

9. He was sleeping on a ship when he was awakened by a frantic captain.

   A. Joel
   B. Paul

C. Jonah

D. Jesus

E. Leonardo DiCaprio

10. He was bound with chains, and sleeping between two soldiers, when an angel appeared in the cell, woke him up, and released him.

    A. Peter

    B. Ezekiel

    C. Paul

    D. Jacob

    E. None of the above

11. He wanted to kill Saul as he slept, but David would not allow it.

    A. Jonathan, son of Saul

    B. Abishai, son of Zeruiah

    C. Ahimelech the Hittite

    D. Acish, son of Maoch

    E. Pistol, son of Gun

12. While sleeping off his exhaustion after losing a fierce battle, Sisera, an army commander, was killed by this woman.

    A. Jael, wife of Heber

    B. Jezebel

    C. Deborah, a judge of Israel

    D. Acsah, daughter of Caleb

    E. Lizzie Borden (a tough ax to follow)

13. As Jesus and the apostles tried to cross a lake in a boat, they found themselves in the midst of a squall. At the time, Jesus was sleeping on a cushion. Which of the disciples went to wake Jesus?

    A. Peter

    B. James and John

C. They all did (none are specifically named)

D. Thomas

E. None—he awoke on his own

14. Which of the following is true concerning Samson, Delilah, and sleep?

    A. Each time Samson told Delilah how his strength could be removed, she attempted to follow the instructions while he slept.

    B. Delilah only managed to get Samson to sleep once, but it was then that she shaved his head, rendering him powerless.

    C. Samson's eyes were gouged out as he slept, then he was tied up by the Philistines and his head was shaved.

    D. Of the four times that Samson offered the secret of his strength to Delilah, twice he apparently allowed her to test the theory while he was awake.

    E. The truth about Samson's strength was that he was born on the planet Krypton and arrived on earth as a baby. (His secret identity was Clark the Kenite.)

15. According to Proverbs 4, the wicked are robbed of sleep until they do what?

    A. Harm the innocent

    B. Spread evil to their neighbor

    C. Speak perversely

    D. Make someone fall

    E. Count evil sheep

Three, two, one. Hey, stop fooling around! I've got answers on page 368. I SAID . . .

Losing a husband is never easy (sometimes you have to run really fast, right ladies?). Okay, that wasn't funny, because I'm talking about losing a husband for good, leaving a widow behind. And there were plenty of those in the Bible. So, before we close out the workout, let's settle in for

ANOTHER WIDOW TRUE/FALSE QUIZ

___ 1. The book of Ruth tells the story of a widow who ends up being the great-grandmother of King David.

___ 2. The woman in the story of the "widow's mite" actually threw two very small copper coins into the temple treasury.

___ 3. Jezebel, a widow herself, died when she accidentally fell out of a window and was subsequently eaten by dogs.

___ 4. Anna, a prophetess and widow who met Mary and Joseph (and Jesus as a child), never left the temple.

___ 5. Mary, the mother of Jesus, was widowed five years before Jesus' crucifixion, according to the book of Acts.

___ 6. The Lord sent the prophet Elijah to Zarepeth of Sidon, to the house of a widow. Elijah arrived there hungry and thirsty. The widow, instructed by God, had already prepared a feast for him.

___ 7. Judah had a widowed daughter-in-law named Tamar. She used deception to become pregnant with Judah's child as a last resort, since God kept killing her husbands.

___ 8. King David forced ten of his concubines to live as widows.

___9. The first mention of Stephen in the Bible was related to complaints that certain widows were being overlooked by the apostles when food was distributed to the needy.

___10. In 1 Corinthians, Paul stated that the highest calling for widows (especially those of childbearing age) was to remarry as soon as they were able, since God told Noah to "be fruitful and multiply."

___11. Eli the priest had a daughter-in-law who died during childbirth shortly after learning she had become a widow.

___12. Peter rebuked a woman named Tabitha for stealing from the Joppa widows treasury. She died shortly thereafter.

___13. The prophet Haggai compares those who oppress widows to adulterers, sorcerers, and perjurers.

___14. Joab, son of Zeruiah, enlisted a woman from Tekoa to pretend to be a widow, and attempt to fool King Solomon.

___15. James offered just two components to define "pure and faultless religion," and one of them pertained to looking after widows.

Question: If a woman wears sunglasses after her husband has died, would you refer to them as "widow shades"?
I don't know either. Your answers are on page 369.

TOP TEN TIP-OFFS THAT SODOM WAS AN EVIL CITY

10. Sign at entrance to town read: "Welcome to Sodom, home of less than ten righteous men"
9. Children were often seen stoning nuns
8. Town mascot was a mongoose
7. Only residents considered moral were comatose
6. Citizens were mainly politicians and used car salesmen
5. Had a multilevel marketing company for switchblades and cocaine
4. Due to uncertainty, children referred to all women as "Mom," and all men as "Dad"
3. Satan was a member of the local college alumni
2. The pastor of the town's only church was the Grinch
1. Every once in a while, a hockey game would break out

Well, you've nearly conquered the **Zondervan's Great Bible Trivia Workout,** and your finest hour is before you. (That's when you complete this last quiz, pat yourself on the back, then go out and buy ten more copies to give to your friends and family to see if they can do half as good as you did!)

Anyway, speaking of finest hours, let's see how you fare on this last challenge pertaining to the high points and better days of some biblical personnel.

CURTAIN CALL

1. After failing to take Ai on the first try, he led the Israelite army to a victory. Then he followed up with a reading of the law between the mountains of Ebal and Gerizim.

   Answer: _____

2. Part of his "redemption" came when his three friends offered sacrifices for their sins, and he prayed for them.

   Answer: _____

3. Her finest hour may have been when Jesus spoke to her after the resurrection, and she went and reported this to the disciples.

   Answer: _____

4. His curtain call came when King Zedekiah sought his counsel concerning the king's own fate in the face of Jerusalem's upcoming defeat by Babylon.

   Answer: _____

5. Her encore was tied to a well of water in the desert of Beersheba, revealed to her by God.

   Answer: _____

6. Although his many miracles were a tough act to follow, he managed to exit the stage in a whirlwind!

   Answer: _____

7. Although he didn't react favorably, he must have felt some sense of honor after being "deified" in Lystra and referred to as Zeus.

    Answer: _____

8. She found better days after being purchased out of slavery and prostitution by her former husband.

    Answer: _____

9. His covenant with God involved circumcision, and if this could be celebrated at age 99, it might be considered a high point for this guy. His son and entire household also participated. (Do you suppose the neighbors called the police about the party where all of the screaming was going on?)

    Answer: _____

10. This high priest may have gotten to take a bow for finding the Book of the Law and having it delivered to King Josiah.

    Answer: _____

11. His last words recorded by someone else were, "Therefore I want you to know that God's salvation has been sent to the Gentiles, and they will listen!"

    Answer: _____

12. Before he exited the stage he disciplined several men for taking foreign wives, both by beating the men and pulling out their hair.

    Answer: _____

13. The Jerusalem council was the stage for his final recorded speech, focusing on salvation by grace. Paul later criticized him for his inconsistency in favoring Jews over Gentiles.

    Answer: _____

14. She was offered center stage by her drunken husband, the king of Persia, but she decided to pass.

    Answer: _____

15. As a crowd-pleaser, his encore involved turning Jesus over to the mob for execution, then allowing Joseph of Arimathea to claim the body.

    Answer: _____

16. His finale, after a long and colorful life, took place on Mt. Nebo. He died there and God buried him.

    Answer: _____ (Better get this one!)

Check your answers on page 369, and if you behave yourself, I'll throw in one more Top Ten List as a bonus!

. . . and just in case you didn't know, here are the

TOP TEN REASONS GOD CREATED HUMANS

10. Animals were too civilized
9. Gabriel bet him they'd stay celibate
8. Things just didn't seem right without denominationalism
7. The snake didn't have anyone to flimflam
6. He wanted more fruits in the garden
5. The cannibals were starving
4. Cows just couldn't do justice to southern gospel music
3. It seemed like a good idea at the time
2. Needed an alternative theory to creationism
1. Tired of making wings and halos

Now, while our amazing cast of Bible characters is warming up for their huge closing extravaganza, I'd like to share some dos and don'ts for your future exercising regimens. Not only will you feel better, but you'll also be much happier if you . . .

DON'T: **Jump** to conclusions
DO: Get a **kick** out of helping others
DON'T: **Stretch** the truth
DO: **Bend** to avoid confrontation
DON'T: **Run** your mouth before your brain is engaged
DO: **Walk** a mile in the shoes of another person
DON'T: **Jog** your memory to recall others' mistakes
DO: **Sit up** and take notice of all the positive things life has to offer!

Well, it sounds like the orchestra is ready, and now, it's my greatest honor to introduce to you a cast of dozens (sorry, our budget wouldn't allow thousands) of those you've enjoyed meeting in **Zondervan's Great Bible Trivia Workout**. Sit back, relax and enjoy . . .

"DON'T WE MAKE THE GOOD BOOK GOOD!"

Cheers, applause, curtain rises:
Opening: Adam & Eve

Tune: Don't It Make My Brown Eyes Blue (Crystal Gayle)

Eden was a paradise,
Free room and board—that's pretty nice.
I think we understood,
And don't we make the Good Book good!

We had it all, we had it made;
Are you surprised we disobeyed?
Come on, you knew we would—
And don't we make the Good Book
Don't we make the Good Book
Don't we make the Good Book good!

(Applause! Enter **Noah** from stage left.)
"Thank you, Adam and Eve! Maestro, a little traveling music, please!"

Tune: Y.M.C.A (Village People)

One day, God was feeling so grieved
Because no one on the earth still believed —
Except me and my good family of course.
And God said I want a di-vorce. ta ta ta ta ta

He said, build a big brown A-R-K,
Build a big brown A-R-K,
For forty days — I'm gonna make it rain,
Wash them bad guys down the drain.

Build me a big brown A-R-K,
Yeah a big, brown A-R-K,
You can cruise the world —
Over cities and towns —
While everybody drowns.

He said Noah, there is just one more thing
You can do for your God and your King.
You must grant me this one minor wish:
Take two of each bird, beast and fish — ta ta ta ta ta

He said, build a big brown A-R-K,
Build a big brown A-R-K,
For forty days — I'm gonna make it rain,
Wash them bad guys down the drain.

Build me a big brown A-R-K,
Yeah a big, brown A-R-K,
You can cruise the world —
Over cities and towns —
While everybody drowns.

Take 'em all on my brown A-R-K
Save 'em all on my brown A-R-K
In just a few months you'll be settlin' in,

To populate earth again —
But for now it's a brown A-R-K
A big honkin' brown A R K
Noah, you're good, I'm savin' your life —
So grab up your kids and wife! Ta ta ta ta ta !!!!

"Thank you, ladies and gentlemen! Now here's the old patri-arch himself, Abraham!"

Tune: The Way You Do the Things You Do (Smokey Robinson)

Well, I was seventy-five—
God said it's time to leave your clan now—
Said take your nephew and your wife,
Get yourself out of Haran, now.
Just head out on the highway,
Trusting my holy inspiration—
And if you follow my way—
You'll start a great and mighty nation.
Well I coulda went anywhere that I wanted to,
But I could tell—his will's the thing I had to do.
Hoo Hoo, Hoo Hoo.
I went to Canaan in the west;
My nephew Lot went east to Sodom;
I saw the top of the world
While he got stuck in the bottom;
I went to bat for his city,
But God just wouldn't halt, now,
And Lot's wife was kinda pretty,
She advertises Morton Salt now—
Well, I coulda done anything that I wanted to
But I could tell—
His will's the thing I had to do,
His will's the thing I had to do (hoo hoo),
His will's the thing I had to do (hoo hoo).

"Thank you, everyone! Thank you!"
Moses enters from stage right, carrying staff.

Tune: Yellow Submarine (The Beatles)

At the time, that I was born,
Jewish boys were to be drowned,
So they hid me in the reeds,
By Pharaoh's daughter, I was found.

I've just lived like a man with low esteem,
A man with low esteem,
A man with low esteem.
I've just lived like a man with low esteem,
A man with low esteem,
A man with low esteem.

When recruited by a bush
To go and set — the Hebrews free,
I dug in, and opted out;
Who would ever — listen to me?
I've just lived like a man with low esteem,
A man with low esteem,
A man with low esteem.
I've just live like a man with low esteem,
A man with low esteem,
A man with low esteem.

After plagues, of many kinds
Pharaoh's mind — began to snap;
So we wandered forty years;
Bad directions — crummy map!

I've just lived like a man with low esteem,
A man with low esteem,
A man with low esteem (everybody!).
I've just lived like a man with low esteem,
A man with low esteem,
A man with low esteem.

"Wow, folks, look who's coming—it's Jeremiah, Ezekiel, Isaiah and Jonah. Let's hear it for 'The Four Prophets.'"

Tune: We Are the Champions (Queen)

Jeremiah

I've wandered around,
As one broken man,
Seeing my people sin —
Babylon kicking our can

Ezekiel

And I've been God's watchman —
Living my own twilight zones,
And I've had these visions of creatures and wheels
And a valley of bones

All

Everybody listen, listen, listen!
We are the prophets of old,
Just tryin' to do as we're told —
We're not out to scorn ya,
We just want to warn ya,
It's time to repent now,
Cause we've all been sent now . . .
By the Lord.

Isaiah

If being a prophet
Is not hard enough —
In order to make a point I spent three years
Walking around in the buff.

Jonah

Though one-upping your story
Is not what I'd planned to do,
I tell you Isaiah you have no idea what it smells like
Inside of Shamu!

Everybody hear us, hear us, hear us.

We are the prophets of old,
And we've known the heat and the cold,
Exiled and beaten,
Yet we kept repeatin'
Righteous responses — cause we are the prophets —
Of old.

(Huge ovation, great signs and wonders!)

Isaiah

"Hey, here come the apostles. This must mean the New Testament, just like I predicted!"

Jeremiah

"It is them, if Isaiah so myself!"

Isaiah

"You're right, Jeremiah . . . you are sad."

Disciples

Tune: Margaritaville (Jimmy Buffet)

Peter, Andrew, James, John

Watchin' our fish nets,
Thinkin' of sunsets,
When this guy calls out "Come follow me!"
Somethin' about him,
Just couldn't doubt him,
Look at us now, we made history.

All

Hastened away right then to do the Master's will
For a chance to be the salt of the earth;
Made our mistakes but that's the chance that one
  takes,
Just to find — to find out what you're worth.

You just have to love us,
All dozen of us,
Though it's a fact that we all have our flaws —
Like Judas the liar,
And Pete the denier,
And while Jesus prayed we all snored like saws.

But still we
Hastened away again to do the Master's will,
For a chance to be the salt of the earth;
Made our mistakes but that's the chance that one
  takes,
Just to find — to find out what you're worth.

It's such a great feeling
When you've finished a healing —
Or fed a big crowd with a couple of perch;
Sending pigs all a screamin'
Cause you filled 'em with demons,
Now there's somethin' you won't see in church!

Gotta hasten away again to do the Master's will,
For a chance to be the salt of the earth —
Made our mistakes but that's the chance that one
   takes,
Just to find — to find out what your worth.

(Loud clapping, whistles, etc.)

Peter

"Okay, everyone come on out—Adam, Eve, Moses, Abraham, the Four Prophets, it's time for the grand finale!"

Reprise: Don't it Make My Brown Eyes Blue

We were good, and we were bad,
Sometimes happy, sometimes sad,
And misunderstood—
But don't we make the Good Book good?

We showed love—we showed rage,
Actors on—God's ancient stage,
Doin' the best we could—
And don't we make the Good Book
Don't we make the Good Book
Don't we make the Good Book good.

We hope you enjoyed your time with us here,
Keep us in memory, and we won't disappear;
Let us make it perfectly clear,
We know we're not great, but we're sure sincere—

The end's in sight, our time is through,
Along with Brad, our thanks to you—
Ovation if you would—
Cause don't we make the Good Book
Don't we make the Good Book
Don't we make the Good Book gooooood!!!

All bow.
(Standing ovation, applause, more applause.)
The curtain closes.

A final thank you for being part of **Zondervan's Great Bible Trivia Workout**. I can see that you're already much better toned than you were when you first bought this book. Way to go! **You'll always be my hero!**

Moses has left the building. Please drive carefully. Goodnight.

Hey—No Peeking!
Pages 321-324

1. D. (Ezek. 16:1–2, 36)
2. E. (Hos. 2:3)
3. B. (Matt. 27:35)
4. A. (Gen. 9:20–22)
5. D. (Amos 2:16)
6. C. (Luke 8:27)
7. B. (Isa. 47:1–3)
8. B. (Gen. 3:6–10)
9. B, E. (Rev. 16:15)
10. D. (Rom. 8:35)
11. A. (Hab. 2:15)
12. C. (Exod. 20:26)
13. D. (2 Sam. 6:20–23)
14. A. (Isa. 20:1–4)

Way to Go, Mo!
Pages 325-327

1. True (Num. 10:29–33)
2. True (Num. 11:13–15)
3. False (Num. 11:31–34)
4. False (Num. 12:1)
5. False (Num. 12:10–15)
6. False (Num. 13:30; see also 14:6–9)
7. True (Num. 14:1–4, 10–20)
8. True (Num. 14:37–38)
9. False (Num. 16:41)
10. True (Num. 17:1–8)
11. According to "oral tradition," this is correct.
12. True (Num. 18:1–7)
13. True (Num. 20:1–11)
14. True (Num. 20:14–21)
15. False (Num. 20:23–29)
16. False (Num. 22:1–6)
17. False (Deut. 7:1–5)
18. True (Deut. 17:14–20)
19. True (Deut. 20:10–15)

20. True (Deut. 31:19–22, 30; 32:1–44)
21. False (Deut. 34:5–6)
22. True (Deut. 34:12)

Order in the Court!
Pages 328-331

Group One
1. Saul
2. Ish-Bosheth
3. David
4. Adonijah (briefly)
5. Solomon (who later had Adonijah killed)
6. Rehoboam

Group Two
1. Rehoboam
2. Abijah
3. Asa
4. Jehoshaphat
5. Jehoram
6. Ahaziah
7. Athaliah (queen)
8. Joash
9. Amaziah
10. Azariah
11. Jotham
12. Ahaz
13. Hezekiah
14. Manasseh
15. Amon
16. Josiah
17. Jehoahaz
18. Jehoiakim
19. Jehoiachin
20. Zedekiah

Group Three
1. Jeroboam I
2. Nadab
3. Baasha

4. Elah
5. Zimri
6. Tibni
7. Omri
8. Ahab
9. Ahaziah
10. Joram
11. Jehu
12. Jehoahaz
13. Jehoash
14. Jeroboam II
15. Zechariah
16. Shallum
17. Menahem
18. Pekahiah
19. Pekah
20. Hoshea

He Says, She Says
Pages 332-337

1. B. (Esther 5:3–4)
2. D. (Matt. 15:21–27)
3. C. (Gen. 16:7–8)
4. B. (Acts 5:8)
5. C. (Job 2:9–10)
6. A. (1 Sam. 25:40–41)
7. C. (Mark 6:22–25)
8. D. (Ruth 3:7–10)
9. A. (Luke 10:40–41)
10. B. (1 Sam. 28:12–13)
11. B. (Gen. 3:13)
12. A. (Judg. 4:6–8)
13. D. (John 4:17–19)
14. C. (Song of Sol. 2:1–2)
15. D. (2 Sam. 6:20–21)

It's a Deal!
Pages 339-340

1. Abraham (Abram), Lot (Gen. 13:8–9)
2. Paul, Barnabas (Acts 15:36–41)
3. Artaxerxes, Nehemiah (Neh. 2:1–6)
4. David, Bathsheba (1 Kings 1:5–40)
5. Legion, Jesus (Mark 5:1–13)
6. Jacob, Laban (Gen. 30:31–34)
7. Nations (or peoples), beast (Rev. 17:15–17)
8. Jonathan, David (1 Sam. 18:3–4)
9. Judas, chief priests (Matt. 26:14–16)
10. Scoffers (or rulers in Jerusalem) death (or the grave) (Isa. 28:14–15)
11. Gamaliel, Sanhedrin (Acts 5:33–40)
12. Gibeonites, Joshua (Josh. 9:1–21)
13. Ananias, Sapphira (Acts 5:1–2)
14. Jews, Paul (Acts 23:12–13)
15. Abraham, Melchizedek (Heb 7:1–4)

Enter the Sandman
Pages 341-344

1. D. (1 Kings 18:27)
2. C. (Luke 22:39)
3. B. (Dan. 6:16–20)
4. B. (1 Sam. 3:2–10)
5. D. (Luke 8:49–56)
6. A. (Gen. 31:40–41)
7. D. (2 Sam. 11:9)
8. D. (Acts 16:26–27)
9. C. (Jon. 1:5–6)
10. A. (Acts 12:6–10)
11. B. (1 Sam. 26:6–12)
12. A. (Judg. 4:17–22)
13. C. (Luke 8:22–24)
14. D. (Judg. 16:4–21)
15. D. (Prov. 4:16)

Another Widow True/False Quiz
Pages 345-346

1. True (Ruth 1:1–5, 4:13–22)
2. True (Mark 12:41–43)
3. False (2 Kings 9:30–37)
4. True (Luke 2:36–38)
5. False (No such account)
6. False (1 Kings 17:7–16)
7. True (Gen. 38:1–30)
8. True (2 Sam. 20:3)
9. True (Acts 6:1–6)
10. False (1 Cor. 7:8–9)
11. True (1 Sam. 4:17–22)
12. False (Acts 9:36–43)
13. False (Mal. 3:5)
14. False (2 Sam. 14:1–21)
15. True (James 1:27)

Curtain Call
Pages 348-350

1. Joshua (Josh. 7:1–8:35)
2. Job (Job 42:7–9)
3. Mary Magdalene (John 20:10–18)
4. Jeremiah (Jer. 38:14–28)
5. Hagar (Gen. 21:14–20)
6. Elijah (2 Kings 2:11)
7. Barnabas (Acts 14:11–18)
8. Gomer (Hos. 3:2–3)
9. Abraham (Gen. 17:23–27)
10. Hilkiah (2 Kings 22:8–10)
11. Paul (Acts 28:28–31)
12. Nehemiah (Neh. 13:23–27)
13. Peter (Acts 15:7–11; Gal. 2:11–21)
14. Vashti (Esther 1:1–12)
15. Pilate (Luke 23:1–25, 50–52)
16. Moses (Deut. 34:1–7)